An Odyssey
of
Becoming
That Summer of '72

Barry and Bobby's
True Adventure

Celeste Gauthier Johnson
with Bobby Young

The Three Tomatoes Book Publishing

Published
ISBN: 979-8-9903014-2-9

Library of Congress Control Number: 2024912972

This work depicts actual events in the lives of the two main characters as truthfully as recollection permits.

For information address:
The Three Tomatoes Book Publishing
6 Soundview Road
Glen Cove, NY 11542

Cover and interior design: Susan Herbst

Dedication

To all the free spirits of the '60s and '70s

Table of Contents

PREFACE

THIS STORY BELONGS TO BARRY and Bobby. I am simply the quilter, the one who organizes and sews each piece of fabric of their journey into a beautiful quilt. In other words, if left to them the squares of material would still be left in a pile, fifty years later.

Through the years, Barry and Bobby have been entertaining friends and strangers, young and old, with their hitchhiking exploits along the Trans-Canada Highway during the summer of '72. Year, time, or place never mattered; when they were together, the stories would flow. And their grand adventure, frozen in time, was the seal of a long-lasting friendship. Inevitably, each time they related a story, they would look at each other and say, "Man, we need to write this down; we need to write a book."

Once I retired, I soon learned that the "we" meant "me." I never tired of hearing about their cross-country adventures. The most memorable story I've heard time and time again has been about Barry and Bobby's encounter with pure malevolence and their brush with death, an incident that took place well into their journey. I shudder to think of what my life would have been like without my husband, Barry.

Twice a week, Barry, Bobby, and I would meet to gather information about their four-week experiences, first hitchhiking and then hopping freight trains. Needless to say, it was not an easy task, necessitating a lot of nagging on my part to stay with the subject at hand. No doubt, the frozen mugs of Beck's beer didn't help the situation, but they would beg to differ. In hindsight, I must say, the tedium of taping, stopping, and re-taping their narratives after each digression from the original outline often transformed me into a ghastly ogre of lore. I can still hear myself saying, totally frustrated and with an elevated voice, "Stick to the story!"

Barry earned himself the title of researcher to ensure accuracy of the logistics of the story and eventually felt confident enough to write down his own thoughts. But more importantly, the book would never have materialized if it wasn't for Barry's dogged determination to make the second trip happen after their failed first attempt that summer. Bobby has always been a keen storyteller with a good long-term memory. Even today as a seventy-two-year-old, he can spin a tale. I found Bobby to be quite a proficient writer himself, so trying to merge some of our texts was beyond difficult. When a story burned so vividly in his brain, literally writing itself on the page, I had to acquiesce and let him take the reins.

But make no mistake about it, this is a collaboration.

INTRODUCTION

WHEN BARRY AND BOBBY SET off on their transcontinental adventure in '72, they were very much a product of the early boomer generation born not long after WWII. The '70s were a time of drugs, sex, and rock 'n' roll. Acid and marijuana were plentiful, the motto Make Love, Not War was still the mantra, bell-bottoms, tie-dye, long hair, and great music were everywhere. It was also a time when young people began to question societal norms and challenged the status quo. Women were fighting for equality; the civil rights battles, and the right to breathe clean air never lost momentum; and the Vietnam war had caused painful divisions even among its youth. The rift between the government and its youth widened in the spring of '70 when the National Guard fired into a crowd at Kent State, killing four and wounding nine. The summer of '72 was the year that White House operatives were arrested for burglarizing the offices of the Democratic National Committee—the start of the Watergate scandal that led to the resignation of President Nixon. And hitchhiking fascinated many young people who donned their backpacks and took off on foot with thumbs out for adventures across the continent in the U.S. and Canada.

Barry and Bobby's attempt to hitchhike cross-country to California and then later through Canada wasn't some impulsive move, but rather was fashioned by the ripeness of the times and their experiences with family, friends, and acquaintances. Barry and Bobby were molded by the different circumstances they were born into, but their commonalities and the generation they were born into ultimately drew them together.

Barry Johnson, born in '52, grew up in an all-white middle-class suburban neighborhood in Holden, a small town bordering the city of Worcester, Massachusetts. He is the youngest of three, the only boy and the only sibling with a freckled face, blue eyes, and red hair. He was always teased about being the milkman's son, a standard joke at the time. His days were spent exploring the woods behind his house, fishing in the nearby brook, and playing sports.

Barry was no stranger to hitchhiking. His first experience was when he was in junior high school. A friend introduced him to golfing, which became his passion at the time. The only problem was the country club was twenty miles away, but that did not deter Barry. With no transportation to get to the country club, his thumb became the simple answer. Hitchhiking with a small outdated early '50s golf bag holding only the essential clubs made it easier for him to catch rides with much older golfers wanting to know more about a thirteen-year-old boy hitchhiking so far away from home to play golf. Back in '65, people never thought twice about picking up hitchhikers and, according to Barry, there was never a lull in the conversation from Holden to Petersham.

Bobby Young made his entrance into this world on Halloween night in '51. He is olive-skinned, brown-eyed, and his smile is defined by a gap between his two front teeth. Like Barry, he is the youngest of three. However, unlike Barry, he lived in Worcester, a city composed of towering three-deckers. Bobby's life was cast into years of harshness and sadness. His mother got pregnant at fifteen and was wed to his dad in a hastily arranged shotgun wedding. It took sixteen years before she had the courage to divorce her abusive alcoholic husband, who terrorized everyone under his roof. The only lingering positive image Bobby has of his dad is his mechanical genius. He credits him for his own mechanical expertise and passion for cars and motorcycles.

Single and divorced, with little income, his mom was forced to move the family often. Bobby moved eight times in just a few years, and with each relocation came a new school. During his darkest days living in poverty, he was encouraged when his mom told him about a scholarship being offered at a prestigious private boarding school in Harrisville, New Hampshire. He took the exam, passed, and was accepted but chose to stay for only one year.

Barry and Bobby became friends under the most unusual circumstances, but then again, it was the '70s. Two years before meeting Barry, Bobby had befriended a sixty-year-old woman named Alice, who offered to give him work and allowed him to pitch his tent behind her house. One summer night around midnight Barry and his friend Bruce were roaming the neighborhood trippin' on "Orange Sunshine." Bruce told Barry that he wanted him to meet his friend, Bobby, so they walked less than a mile up the narrow country road and approached Bobby's tent from the woods. When they opened the tent flaps, they saw Bobby lying there in his makeshift bed moaning and groaning. All Barry could think of was, *This isn't going to be a good trip!*

It was evident Bobby needed medical attention, and neither guy was in any condition to take him to a hospital. To make matters worse, Alice had just finished drinking a big bottle of wine. They could have called 911, but of course, no one was thinking very clearly.

What they didn't know was that during that day, Bobby had been on a boating trip with his girlfriend, Christine, who had made tuna salad sandwiches for lunch. Her sandwich was on the bottom of the Styrofoam ice chest while Bobby's sandwich sat in the sun for hours. After dropping Christine off at her house, the drama began. Bobby's stomach was in turmoil, with incredible gas pains. Sweating. Heaving. His arms were locked, crisscrossed against his chest and he was unable to straighten them out.

Barry remembered not being able to take his eyes off Bobby as he begged them to straighten out his cramped arms, but they just gawked at him, too high to process what was happening. All Barry could think of was, *Wow! Look at the pain on his face!*

Finally, after a few minutes, Barry and Bruce decided to wake Alice and tell her about Bobby. She gave them some small indigestion pills to give to Bobby, but that didn't work so they ran off to see Alice again. She gave Bruce the keys to her van to take him to the hospital ASAP.

Bruce, white-knuckled at the wheel and hyper-focused on the road, drove at what seemed to be twenty miles an hour. They brought Bobby into the emergency room behind the hospital, Barry holding up Bobby on one side and Bruce holding him on the other. A nurse approached them and asked what was going on, squinting, shifting her beady brown eyes toward Bobby and then to the guys who were tripping. When she turned to ask Bobby a few questions, the guys silently slithered out the door.

Poor Bobby, suffering from what they later learned was food poisoning, did not fare very well among the five other patients in the ward. As soon as the nurse learned that Bobby had taken the little red pills for "indigestion," Florence Nightingale turned into Nurse Ratchet.

A friendship slowly evolved. Bobby somehow always felt that

his friends saved his life that memorable night from hell. On Memorial Day weekend, Barry and Bobby planned a motorcycle trip to Cape Cod, Massachusetts. There they discovered they had a lot in common — motorcycles, the spirit of adventure, and the company of girls. They liked the idea that neither of them needed much to survive. They could go days without eating.

When Barry learned his good friend Donnie B. was heading to California, he asked him if he and his friend Bobby could tag along until they reached the Mississippi River, and then they would hitchhike the rest of the way. A "yes" from Donnie set the plan in motion, and even though one might call it a failure, in hindsight, it prepared them for their next trip on the Trans-Canada Highway.

The narrative you are about to read is not a "hero's journey" but simply a story of two young men coming of age in an era that allowed them to do so.

PART I

The one thing I miss is hitchhiking. Now there's no more of that. When's the last time you saw a hitchhiker? It's not that I consider it a great sport, but it was my way of seeing the country.
The open road, especially in the western United States, is still very pristine, but everything else around it has changed.

~ Edward Ruscha

Chapter 1

A NEW VENTURE BEGINS

AND SO THE STORY BEGINS... after the failed cross-country hitchhiking attempt to California earlier in June, Barry contacted Bobby and asked him if he would be willing to try again. Bobby, content to be home with his girlfriend, Christine, declined the offer.

"Let me know if you change your mind."

On some level, Bobby was still toying with the idea of taking that trip with Barry, but he also knew it was important to nurture his relationship with Christine, and they had already planned a motorcycle trip to Maine.

Meanwhile, the gnawing in Barry's gut never subsided, especially when he had missed the opportunity to go to Woodstock, where the iconic concert gathering of all time took place. He never lost his desire to travel across the country to the West Coast, and for him, the sooner, the better. While working at the college bookstore, he happened to peruse through a *Whole Earth Catalog*. His attention was drawn to the information about hostels and how Canada's youth were encouraged to hitchhike. The hostels, based on the European model, were scattered all along the Trans-Canada Highway. Barry was intrigued by the Canadian government's way of thinking. For Canadians, it was a benefit to society if their children knew more about their country. That said, they never discouraged travel and actually promoted their youths' exploration by financing hostels to provide food and safe lodging.

The United States, however, had a different outlook on the topic of hitchhiking. They didn't provide hostels. Furthermore, there was no consistency in state laws for hitchhiking, so it could be legal in some states but not in others. Also, adults frowned upon the culture of kids with long hair, who just didn't fit into the values that they had growing up in a different era. Consequently, Canada was a beacon to the very soul of those filled with wanderlust and a spirit of adventure.

A week and a half later, after returning from his motorcycle trip, Bobby called Barry to tell him he was willing to try again. This time, Barry insisted they travel by way of the Trans-Canada Highway. Wisdom and hindsight from their first trip gave them the confidence to move forward and prepare themselves for the problems and challenges that may lie ahead. Planning had become strategic. This time, they rid themselves of any unnecessary gear: pup tent, fishing pole, and camera. Instead, they loaded up their external aluminum-framed backpacks with the essentials: sleeping bags, space blankets, mess kit, canteens, one miniature fold-up Sterno stove, toothbrushes, toothpaste, toilet paper, underwear, socks, canned goods, and, of course, boxes of Kraft Mac & Cheese. More importantly, Barry tucked a Rand McNally atlas of the United States and Canada into his backpack. By mid-July, each with a hundred dollars, Bobby's in cash and Barry's in traveler's checks plus thirty-five dollars in cash, they boarded a Peter Pan bus at the Trailways bus station in Worcester, Massachusetts. Destination: Montreal, Canada.

Once on the bus, Barry felt a sense of relief, but sleep was unattainable as a swirl of images of his first trip gave him no rest.

From the beginning of the summer, having just graduated from Quinsigamond Community College in Worcester, he had an insatiable desire to travel. He had yearned for adventure. Sinking back into his seat now, he closed his eyes, and invited the scenes of his first trip to emerge.

He remembered his friend, Mark S., coming home with stories about hitchhiking to California. His friend Donnie, with his girlfriend, Mary, as well as his friend Paul and his girlfriend, Karen, had planned a cross-country trip. Barry had asked Donnie if he and his friend Bobby could join them. Donnie said, "Sure." Their agreement was to ride with Donnie as far as the Mississippi River, a two- or three-day ride, and then start hitching.

Being in such close quarters on the highway, Barry could not help but notice how Donnie and Paul were so strikingly different. Donnie was a sergeant in the Green Berets, commanding a platoon of Montagnard tribesmen in what would only later become known as Operation Tailwind, a military secret mission into Laos in the Vietnam War in '70. Donnie and sixteen other Green Berets were part of that Special Operations, a clandestine mission Barry wouldn't know anything about until it was declassified in 2017. Barry smiled to think of Donnie now, his dark-bearded, long-haired, pot-smoking friend. Conversely, Paul, who was also a Vietnam vet, kept his hair well-groomed, his clothes neat, and was a cut above the rest of them. Later, he was involved in the stock market. Over the course of the next fifteen years, he developed his trading skills and became the leader in the eventual takeover in '87 of Singer, originally a sewing company, which had diversified to include office equipment, defense, and aerospace.

Barry looked around Donnie's '69 robin's-egg blue Dodge window van, a US government surplus van to be exact. Donnie had purchased the van as soon as he was discharged from the Green Berets. Problems with "Old Bluebird" never ceased. On previous camping trips, Donnie frequently had problems with the van—alternator problems, battery problems, you name it. With the battery constantly overcharging and boiling, "Old Bluebird" couldn't go over fifty miles an hour. These problems were compounded with the dead weight brought on by two extra travelers and their packs.

After the little ninety HP engine ceased for the evening, they all spent the night in a picnic area at Raymond B. Winter State Park Campground in Pennsylvania. Barry decided to try his hand at fishing for trout when he heard shouting. Thinking it was the game warden, and being a bit paranoid since he was fishing without a license, he ran off, stubbing his toe on a rock, a bane that would torment him for the rest of the trip. He found himself hobbling around with a throbbing toe, and no fish to show for his efforts. Bobby had incurred his own issues, a painful burgeoning urinary tract infection. Now it was becoming apparent that Bobby's infection was worsening and would need medical attention soon.

After a fitful night's sleep, Bobby told Barry that he wasn't doing well and needed to go to a hospital. Barry related the message to Donnie who said, "No problem." The nearest hospital was in Lafayette, Indiana. As promised, he dropped them off in front of the emergency room.

When Bobby entered the hospital, he gave the staff a fictitious name, so he wouldn't be billed. After a shot of penicillin and a prescription to go, he left the hospital. Renewed in spirit and ready to begin their journey, they got on the road with thumbs extended. Later, a man in a pickup truck stopped and told them to jump in the back. The driver dropped them off at a truck stop in a small town, surrounded by cornfields, where they were happy to take a shower and get something to eat.

The bus squealed to a stop, and Barry's reverie was broken. The five-hour ride was uneventful, that is until Bobby encountered an unexpected snag at the border. Upon reaching Canada, all passengers had to disembark per order of border patrol. Emigration was on high alert, looking for "draft dodgers," which was a routine practice since the Vietnam War. Barry was pushed through without incident. Bobby, on the other hand, was not so lucky. He was pulled out of the line for further scrutiny. Even though it was a random selection, he found it unsettling.

A year prior, he showed up at the draft registration office (a few months late) to register for the draft. He handed his paperwork to the uniformed woman behind the desk. Their exchange went like this:

After a quick glance, she intoned icily, "You do realize you are four months late for registering."

"Yep!" he replied belligerently.

Clearing her throat and with cold eyes boring into him she said flatly, "Considering your delinquency, your case will be given special attention."

Bobby's temper boiled over. "My brother just spent a month in St. Albans's Naval Hospital with a gunshot through his kidney and my cousin just came home in a body bag." Before she could say another word, he turned on his heel and walked out the door.

This incident was on his mind as he was sent to a secure windowed room with wire-enmeshed security glass. A man from U.S. Immigration had a catalog of named draft dodgers and was looking to see if the name Robert Young was listed.

Outside the room, the bus driver, who kept glancing at his watch, was growing anxious. He turned and said, "Excuse me, officer, I have a schedule to keep. Everyone has passed through security except the young man in the interrogation room. I can't wait much longer."

"I will see what I can do," said the border patrol agent. The immigration officer knocked on the interrogation room door and spoke to the interrogator. And just like that, Bobby was boarding the bus without further objection.

Chapter 2

PRINCIPLES OF HOSTELS 101 AND A TRIBUTE TO TRUCK DRIVERS

ONCE THEY STEPPED OFF THE bus in Montreal, finding the hostel was front and center on their minds. The hostel they came upon the first night was an old YMCA gymnasium with rows and rows of army cots. Adjacent to the gymnasium there was a locker room and a facility where the guests could bathe. At this particular hostel the caretakers were not overly friendly and encouraged everyone to speak French.

Waking up in a hostel the first morning was quite ordinary, yet it held some intrigue given that it was a novel experience. The guys discussed their plans for the day over a typical breakfast of cereal, milk, toast, peanut butter, and grape jelly. Bobby and Barry were cautious and took turns taking a shower to safeguard their belongings. Bobby always gets a laugh or two when he entertains listeners with his Fruit of the Loom anecdote. As he was getting out of the shower clad in his underwear, a Canadian who spoke English pointed to Bobby and with a heavy French accent yelled, "You are an American, eh?"

Bobby, not sure how he should respond to the guy's half statement, half question asked, "How do you know?"

With a hearty laugh the Canadian responded, "Because of

your white underwear, eh?"

Bobby became self-conscious. Geez, not even twenty-four hours had passed, and his cover was blown. Yes, he was an American.

The mixture of impatience, anticipation, and the thrill of what lay ahead was mounting. Having gained knowledge about the Trans-Canada hostel circuit from fellow travelers, they concluded their target for the day would be North Bay.

Hitching out of Montreal, they were picked up by a truck driver, who made it clear that the duo's sole purpose was to keep him awake. Bobby, who had a keen interest in big machines and how they worked, kept asking the old truck driver questions throughout the ride. The seasoned driver enjoyed teaching Bobby about his "4070A International Transtar tractor trailer truck with a 318 Detroit and 13-speed." Meanwhile, Barry, noted for his bouts of car sickness unless he is sitting in the front seat, jumped into the bunk, found his niche, and instantly fell into a deep slumber.

Barry and Bobby didn't fare as well on their second night having arrived at the hostel in North Bay after the curfew. They had a feeling this would happen, but they pounded on the green wooden door anyway to no avail. The hope of anyone opening the locked doors was unlikely. They looked at each other with a long sigh.

The first word coming from Barry was, "Fuck!" Then pointing to the bushes he asked, "What da ya think? Stay there tonight?"

Looking at his backpack and pulling out his space blanket, Bobby gestured to the fence, and said, "It looks like a good place to me. We'll be safe and secure being on-site."

Adding to their misery, rain began to fall in a steady drizzle. Undeterred and needing to rest, they jumped a low fence, found a dry place, covered themselves with a space blanket, and settled in for the night.

On day three, they hitched a ride with another truck driver heading west to Sudbury. As with each person behind the wheel, a story, a lesson, or a bit of information was always a part of the ride. At the time Sudbury was a unique mining town, noted primarily for extracting copper, palladium, platinum group elements, and nickel. In fact, it was noted to have the ninth deepest nickel mine in the world. Additionally, it was home to unparalleled towering smokestacks, and to no one's surprise, sources of toxic waste.

Traveling along the Trans-Canada Highway, there were telltale signs they were getting close to Sudbury; the trees looked like they were dying. Nearing closer, all that remained were serrated timbers and jagged stumps, until finally—nothing, just a cemetery of dead trees. To combat the pollution produced by smelting, the folks built a higher stack, 1,250 feet, next to the first one to push the smoke farther up into the sky and move it farther downwind, a decision impacting human and plant life in the future.

The driver wished the guys well before dropping them off near the truck stop diner located on the north side of the road, east of Sudbury. A strip mine was across the street. Some people have speculated it might have been a hill in its day. Miners stripped it off, leaving a hole in the ground, where the spoils from the mine were scattered around the whole area. Often, miners would look for veins, solid chunks, and would begin digging for whatever they thought was valuable. Whatever was not valuable was just left there in a heap.

When they reached the diner, they looked around in stunned silence. All they could see were miles and miles of rubble—rock, pebbles, and dirt.

"Man, it looks like a moonscape," said Barry. "There isn't even a speck of green anywhere."

"Yeah, this diner should be called Moonscape Diner," quipped

Bobby.

As they walked through the parking lot to go into the eatery, they saw four or five school buses painted gray, transporting the miners from wherever they had parked their cars to work the mines. Before being bused to the quarry, the men would stop at the diner to have breakfast. Barry and Bobby walked inside, nodded to the group of miners, and sat at the counter.

Curious about the town, they struck up a conversation with the waitress, a fifty-year-old woman born and raised in Sudbury. The drab grayness of her hair matched the terrain from which she stood. In a gruff voice she asked, "What'll ya have, boys?"

Before placing an order, Bobby asked, "Why is everything so deserted and dead?"

Millie, the waitress, reiterated what the truck driver had told them. She then took a moment. Laying her hand on the counter, looking at them, but not really seeing them, she said, "When I was a young girl there used to be green plants—grass, shrubs, flowers, trees...but they died over time because of all the mining." The images of green now evaporating, she looked at the guys and went on to say, "Soon the ground was so toxic that efforts to restore the landscape long after the devastation was near impossible."

Who knows what propelled her to continue with her wasteland saga. "The people in town"—a smoker's cough interrupted her mid-sentence — "were concerned about the pollution the smokestacks were pouring out, so they built another that is even higher next to the original. This new one is about a quarter of a mile high and the second highest stack in the world. Hopefully, it will push up the smoke and carry it out of this town. We need to start seeing green again."

She stood straight, took her pen and pad in hand, and once again said, "What'll ya have, boys?"

The words of the waitress jolted a memory as Barry headed out of Sudbury. A few years prior he remembered camping in the Adirondack Mountains in New York State and seeing a crystal-clear lake. But, to his dismay, the only remaining fish were suckers where trout should have been. He always wondered if Sudbury could have been a contributing factor.

Chapter 3

A MEMORY OF A GOOD DAY TURNED BAD

AFTER A MEAGER BREAKFAST, THEY walked through the restaurant parking lot to the highway and began hitching once again. Bobby viewed it first, looked at Barry, and said, "Here comes a cop." The sight of the cruiser gave rise to a torrent of unwanted memories of their first hitchhiking trip. It was well understood at the time: Bobby and cops don't mix. Their previous ill-fated trip the month before, when they were just outside the Illinois state line, did not start off well.

Their memory was still vivid. It was afternoon, three weeks before, when they stopped for food. Bobby paid his bill and was pleasantly surprised when he counted his change and discovered the waitress had given him an extra ten dollars, an unexpected gift, a "big deal!" They began hitching a ride, and soon they were picked up by a guy in a red pickup truck who dropped them off at the next exit ramp just before the overpass where the driver got off the interstate. They walked underneath the overpass so they could hitchhike in the shade. Unlike Bobby, who was dark-haired with olive skin, Barry was the poster child of a typical Scandinavian. He was half Norwegian with fiery red hair atop a pale, freckled face.

Later in the day, a whopping storm came into view to the southwest and brought mounting winds. They could hear the booming clashes of thunder and see flashes of lightning even though it was miles away on the flat corn-fields.

Barry and Bobby looked at each other and thought, this doesn't look good. Fearing a tornado, they climbed the embankment under the bridge and sought protection there. The wind pushed the pouring rain down in big sheets sideways. Both agreed it was the worst storm they had ever seen. Being from the mountainous regions of New England, they were not used to the unexpected, abrupt intensity of Midwestern storms and were taken completely off guard. As night descended, they welcomed their newfound niche on the concrete plateau. They shouted back and forth over the traffic above them. They were a third of the way to California, and they hoped to get an uninterrupted ride along the way. Eventually, they fell asleep to the drizzling rain and the occasionally rumbling car and trucks.

Rising with the first rays of sunshine, they started hitchhiking again. Almost immediately a state cop traveling in the opposite direction spotted them, spun his car around, and came back to get them. The officer got out of his car, swaggered over to where they stood, and said, "Boys, hitchhiking on the interstate is against the law in Illinois. Turn around and put your hands behind your back."

Bobby felt a range of emotions from apprehension to fear after having had dealings with the police in his past. Barry took it in stride.

They noticed there was another hiker, whom they later learned was named Ralph, already in the back of the cruiser. Ralph had unruly long hair and his jeans and T-shirt were filthy. And, according to Bobby who was placed in the back seat next to him, the odor emanating from his feet was enough to induce spasms of gagging. To make matters worse, because they were handcuffed, they couldn't roll down the windows. As the cruiser approached the sign that read: Welcome to Cambridge, Illinois, the Hog Capital of the World. Ralph began "oinking" loudly, which he kept up until they arrived at the police station. The oinking sound was both an insult to town and cops, who were called "pigs" in the '70s. Ralph's impropriety would come back to haunt them in the near future.

Once inside the police station, they were each allowed to make one phone call. Barry called his mom collect. She wasn't home, but Barry remembered his sister, Melanie, answering the phone and admonishing the officers to do no harm to her baby brother. Barry, Bobby, and Ralph were escorted to the holding tank in the courthouse to await their arraignment. The defense attorney, whom they had never seen before, was pleading their case and suggested a figurative slap on the wrist. Unfortunately, the trooper had placed Barry and Bobby in the same pod as Ralph, who had disrespected the trooper, oinking his way through Cambridge. After a disapproving look from the judge—tsk, tsk, tsk—a stiff penalty of five dollars a day was given. With no money to spare, along with their reluctance to pay a twenty-five-dollar fine, they were carted off to jail for five days.

Barry got his own cell. There was a broken window where birds had built a nest inside the steel mesh. Doomed to misery, Bobby was once again partnered with

Ralph and placed in the same cell. Barry wallowed in his misery by playing his harmonica. The inmates were not amused, and voiced their exasperation in unison, "Shut the fuck up!!" This only incited Ralph, whose greatest pleasure was casting insults back at the inmates.

After a night of fitful sleep, the guys were happy to see the trustees bring in a bland breakfast prepared by the seasoned inmates. They were given scrambled eggs with no utensils. Bobby to this day is convinced the scrambled eggs were sprinkled with what seemed to be shards of glass. Ralph needed his second cup of tea, so he occupied himself by taking the metal end off a light bulb to create a heating element for a teapot. He used toilet paper to form a ring, put it down in the toilet, and lit it on fire somehow. He then made tea using his first teabag from the morning. You might ask yourself, "Did he use toilet water to make the tea?" No, he opted for tap water. Still, one would want to ask, "Why would anyone want to make tea in a toilet bowl?"

Each cellblock contained two cells and a day room enclosed with bars with one picnic table anchored to the floor. These adventure seekers were stuck in the doldrums for two full days. To occupy themselves, Barry played his harmonica and drew an elaborate snake on the picnic table. For physical activity, he climbed the prison bars like a spider monkey. Bobby wrote love letters to his girlfriend, Christine, on toilet paper to occupy his time.

Tensions grew between the guys and the long-term inmates. Bobby was feeling miserable, despondent, and downright ornery.

Three days behind bars in Cambridge in Henry

County was all it took for Bobby to know he wanted to go home. Bobby felt like an active volcano and having saved fifteen dollars by sitting in jail for three days, feeling home-sick and frustrated, and yearning to be with Christine, his anger exploded. At one minute after midnight on the third night, Bobby started his tirade, "Let me out!"

"Shut the fuck up!" shouted the desk cop.

"Get me the fuck outta here!" Bob bellowed as he scraped and banged his cup against the bars.

Inmates added to the cacophony, "Shut the fuck up! I can't sleep, you motherfuckers!"

Barry was awakened by the commotion. He yelled, "Bobby, what's going on?"

Bobby yelled back, "Barry, I need to get out, I need to get out now!"

At the top of the stairs, the desk sergeant bellowed, "What is going on?" Bobby shouted he wanted out and was willing to pay the balance. Barry knew what he need-ed to do. When the cop came to release Bobby, Barry asked to be released too. A half hour later, the cell doors opened; the officer marched them downstairs where they settled up their debt to society. After processing, they gathered their personal belongings and walked out the front door of the red-bricked jail in the town of Cambridge, Illinois. It was close to two in the morning.

Now on the Trans-Canada Highway a month later, Barry was looking at another cop car and could see distress in Bobby's de-meanor. They had a shared history of anxiety—Bobby with cops and Barry with girls—so it became a mutual understanding that Barry would handle the police, and Bobby would take the lead in social situations involving girls.

Barry now looked at his friend, and said, "I got this. Let me do the talking."

The cop stopped, leaned out his window, and asked, "Do you guys want a ride? Hop in."

Feeling they had no choice, and with mild apprehension, they accepted the ride. Barry rode in the front seat, and Bobby jumped in the back.

A casual conversation ensued, as the officer tried to figure out who these guys were and what they were up to. He was older and pretty savvy when it came to judging people. Satisfied with what he had learned, and with a knowing smile, he said, "Well, guys, I am going to give you a ride to the town line." And sure enough, he drove them right through the downtown and just outside the city limits on the west side of Sudbury.

Chapter 4

CANADIAN KINDNESS AND A BIG OLD GOOSE

TRAVELING WITHOUT A SOLID PLAN opened countless possibilities in a single day. West of Montreal in the town of Sault Ste. Marie, they unexpectedly met a girl who had just stepped off a bus. She laid eyes on the boys shouldering backpacks and seemed genuinely interested in them. Bobby seized the moment by initiating a conversation. In one breath, they learned her name was Michelle and she was a seventeen-year-old senior in high school. Learning these guys were American hitchhikers beginning their explorations in Canada piqued her interest. She wanted to know more about them. Comfortable in their presence, she invited them to her apartment.

Upon entering the living room, she told them to make themselves at home and asked them if they wanted a drink. Parched, after a long day in the sun, they nodded. She played Chicago on the phonograph and walked into the kitchen, returning with three ice-filled glasses of Coke. It didn't take long for them to discover that she was not only petite and pretty but very intelligent and inquisitive as well.

During their short stay they were barraged with questions regarding the United States. She wanted to know what they thought about the upcoming McGovern and Nixon election and how they felt about the '70 shooting at Kent State University, where four people were killed. She asked probing questions about the Vietnam War protests since Canada did not participate in the war. Just as she verbalized the word Woodstock, she cast a calculated look at the clock. "Oh man, you guys had better leave. My mom is coming home from work and would not approve of seeing you guys here."

Perfunctorily, hugs were exchanged and as quickly as the bond of friendship was ignited, it was extinguished when the door closed behind them. It became apparent at the moment that the sole purpose of her invitation was all about satisfying her curiosity about life in America. Without so much as a word, they eyed each other and concluded, *Time to get back on the road.*

It was still early afternoon. By day four, thumbing a ride was becoming second nature to them. They stood on the side of the road facing the traffic, made eye contact with every passing car, and with their thumbs extended the process began once again. An old Ford pickup truck passed them and then slowed down to a stop in the breakdown lane. Barry and Bobby hustled up to the truck. The driver told them that they were going as far as Wawa, which means "wild goose" in Ojibwe, and they were welcome to jump in the back of the truck.

The driver was a Chippewa Indian in his early twenties. Barry and Bobby wondered why he looked so happy, his smile filling up the cabin of the old truck. His wife, who sat beside him, had long hair parted in the middle with two long shiny thick black braids. She had given birth at Sault Ste. Marie Hospital a few days prior. Snuggled against her chest lay a tiny infant swaddled in an embroidered Indian blanket mottled with colorful Indian symbols and designs. On the opposite side of her sat a man, presumably a friend, since he was about the same age as the couple. Unlike her husband, who had short hair, he wore a ball cap atop his shoulder-length windblown hair.

Before they drove off and settled in, the driver whose name they coined as "Happy Daddy" yelled, "Hey, hand us a few beers from the case under the canvas tarp. And help yourself."

A two-four box of twenty-four Labatt beers rested between them. In spite of the amount of beer being passed through both the driver and passenger sides of the cab, the speed of the ride, and the cold rain beginning to pour down upon them, Barry and Bobby still maintained a sense of optimism that wherever they were dropped off, they would still be alive. To shield themselves against the biting rain, they pulled the tarp over themselves and leaned against the back of the cab, protecting themselves from the full force of the turbulent, wind-driven, cold rain. After riding for a good two hours, the driver stopped at Wawa since the reservation was in the opposite direction. Needless to say, they both had a good buzz on.

They were dropped off at the junction of the Trans-Canada Highway and Highway 101. They walked to the outskirts of Wawa and then passed through the town, curious to know a little more about the looming Canada Goose. How could you miss it! It was a colossal twenty-eight-foot-tall, twenty-two-foot-long steel goose with a wingspan of twenty feet. The famous Goose was erected in '60 during the same year when the last link of Lake Superior of the Trans-Canada Highway was constructed and obstructed the view of the town. The Goose was made with chicken wire and plaster and deteriorated due to weather conditions. In '63 it was recreated with steel. It was built to remind the tourists Wawa was alive and well. The massive goose had become their symbol of welcome.

Barry did not want to stay in Wawa, especially after learning bits and pieces, stories of stranded hitchhikers, the stuff of urban legends. One legend in particular revolves around a hitchhiker who couldn't get a ride out of Wawa. Subsequently, every day before hitchhiking out in the hopes of catching a ride, he would go into the café, and just sit drinking his coffee. Rumor has it that he went there so often he and the waitress fell in love, got married, and "lived happily ever after" and never left Wawa. After hearing the man's tale, hitchhikers were terrified at the thought of getting stuck in Wawa.

In '71, the Canadian rock band, Crowbar, wrote a song about Wawa titled, "Tits up the Pavement" on the album *Larger than Life* (Daffodil Records). Kelly Jay Fordham, the lead singer for the band, became a legend in his own right. His musical talent and songs infused pride and recognition for the Canadian people.

Outside Wawa, Barry and Bobby hiked for a few hours in the blazing sun with no success. One of them would take a snooze on his backpack in the breakdown lane, while the other one hitched. Finally, whether from boredom or hunger, perhaps both, they pulled out the old Sterno stove, a box of Kraft Mac & Cheese from one of the backpacks and added a can of Vienna sausages to enrich their meal all the while humming "Lodi" by Creedence Clearwater Revival. With the prospect of getting a ride waning, they bedded in the woods for the night, hoping for better luck in the morning.

Chapter 5

FIVE DOLLARS FOR A RIDE

As THE HOURS DRAGGED ON, Barry and Bobby became despondent, and thoughts of being stranded in Wawa for what might be an eternity didn't ease their anxiety. Hitchhiking was very competitive, and there was an unwritten rule: thou shalt not preempt a fellow hitchhiker. It wasn't unusual for hitchhikers to cross each other's traveling path throughout the trip, which created a spirit of camaraderie among the hitchhikers.

That being said, if you saw a fellow hiker next in line for a ride at a junction, "etiquette" required that they would have to wait a distant mile behind him. Desperate to step out of what felt like suspended animation, Barry made signs out of cardboard with the plea: ***FIVE DOLLARS FOR A RIDE***. To enhance their chances of catching a ride, Bobby employed tactical measures. Beginning from where Barry stood, Bobby walked down the breakdown lane and set up three signs against any available rock about 660 feet apart.

Within forty-five minutes, a green '63 Volkswagen rolled its way toward them. "Oh look, it is a Massachusetts plate! They both shouted and waved their arms, "Massachusetts!! Massachusetts!!" The driver looked in his rearview mirror and was probably thinking, *What the hell? Do I know these guys?* He was so curious about their clownish antics that he made a U-turn, stopped, and looked at them quizzically.

"Hey, we're from Worcester, Massachusetts! We're just trying to get out of Wawa."

"Where ya guys headed?"

Barry said, "West, eventually California. We're just looking for the nearest hostel to spend the night."

The couple smiled and the young man said, "Squeeze in."

They could aptly be described as the embodiment of the typical liberal hippies of the '70s, both Harvard grads. He was a young, bearded man with shoulder-length curly brown hair; his girlfriend wore round wire-rimmed glasses. A rectangular blue, magenta, and white paisley scarf was wrapped around her head covering the top of her long black hair. The scene of what came next was both distressing and humorous. Riding with them was an eighty-to-ninety-pound stinky old coonhound. Grateful for the ride, they crammed their stuff and themselves in the back seat with Old Stinky smack between them.

Owing a debt of gratitude, they sat silently sweating profusely in a hot car with no pop-out windows, no sunroof, and definitely no air-conditioning; their sole means of getting access to fresh air was from the front windows. Exacerbating their situation was the fact that the dog wasn't comfortable either; he was fidgeting around. In order to spread out his massive bulk in the limited space, he rested the front half of his body with one front paw on the driver's seat and the other one on the passenger's seat. His smelly half with big balls that swayed with every wag of his massive tail was a constant distraction, not to mention his intermittent puffs of gas. There was little to no conversation. And so it went for the next several hours. The car, weighed down with four adults, all their gear, and a ninety-pound dog traveled at a speed of forty-five miles an hour.

The ride was long, laborious, and lackluster, until...*boom*! The tire blew! In a panic, cultured-hippie-man chaotically wrestled the steering wheel in a desperate attempt to gain control of the violently swerving vehicle. Somehow the car successfully came to a stop in the breakdown lane upright on all four wheels. They were all clearly shaken, including Old Stinky. Exiting the car was not easy for the back seat travelers. But once out of the car, they assessed the damage. True to his nature, Bobby offered to change the tire, and they all rode on as if nothing major had occurred. Thankful for the "kindness of strangers" from Boston, the couple and their dog continued to their reserved destination for the night.

Barry and Bobby were now on Route 102, a side highway off the Trans-Canada highway (highway 17) in North Thunder Bay. From their map, it appeared to be a much shorter route to reconnect, instead of going south through Thunder Bay. It was now late afternoon with still four or five hours more of sunlight. Barry stuck out his thumb with no cardboard destination and almost immediately a car stopped.

They were in for quite an experience when they were picked up by a couple, runaway lovers in their mid-twenties driving a steel gray late '60s model 2002 BMW sedan. (Bobby was able to recall almost every single car he had encountered on the trip.) Canada 1 was not a limited access highway in that it didn't have formal entrances and exits like an American interstate highway, such as U.S. 1 or U.S. 301. Roads and streets would randomly intersect.

When the car stopped, a woman with very long dark bushy hair and bushy eyebrows above deep brown eyes stepped out to greet the guys and motioned them into the backseat of the car. Her dark olive complexion dusted with soft, faint facial hair suggested that she may have been Mediterranean or Italian. She was short, her build thick, but not fat. Her presumed boyfriend or husband was mysteriously quiet, and he let her do all the talking. They had not been riding very long before she announced that they were running away. Not knowing the backstory, Bobby, nonetheless, had the impression based on her nervous tone and somewhat guilty demeanor, that she knew in advance that this tryst would end badly. Apparently, they were not too far from home since they were very familiar with the area.

"Hey, Johnny and I are going for a swim and then catch some rays. Are you guys good with that?"

They both said, "Sure!"

The driver turned off the main road where the asphalt quickly turned into a dirt road. They passed a lone shack, which unbeknown to them at the time, would become their sleeping quarters for the night. It was situated about a mile from Canada 1 and about three miles from their eventual destination, a secluded pond.

As soon as the car was parked, they piled out. She looked at them and asked, "Are you guys 'body conscious?'" She never waited for an answer and if there was one, she paid no attention. She stripped off her clothes and jumped in the water.

Bobby shrugged and Barry smiled. "Why not?"

Johnny was tall and lanky. Black curly hair and a slender beard framed his pasty face. The only color on his sun-deprived body was the thin black hair on his chest. Once they were all stripped and wading through the cold water, Barry and Bobby self-consciously turned to view the naked body before them as they desperately tried to keep their eyes on the scenery. What they saw was a beautifully endowed woman standing in knee-deep water. Her hands were clasped tightly under her chin, elbows in, in reaction to the cold water. Pressed between her forearms was the focus of their attention.

After the unforeseen but delightful swim, they all left the pond area fully dressed. With the promise of being picked up in the morning, Barry and Bobby were dropped off at the outbuilding, first thought of as a shack, a mile or so from Canada 1. At one time the building might have been associated with an old farm, whose house and barn had disappeared long ago. It was well-constructed, meaning that the materials used to build it were durable, evidenced by the fact it was still standing. The door was framed and looked as though it had not been opened in years. With a bit of effort and a grinding scrape, the door gave way. The one-room structure was dank and dusty from many years of decay. They surveyed the room and chose the spot where they would spend the night.

Because they had no food, they resorted to slurping up the packets of ketchup that had been stored in their backpacks. For dessert, they took turns savoring the taste of an old sour ball retrieved from the bottom of one of the backpacks and passed it back and forth. Having had little food for most of the trip, their stomachs had shrunk so they were satisfied with the little nourishment they had. Plus, now the guys had something completely different to focus their attention on—namely, Lady Godiva.

Barry was first to broach the topic. "Man, I can't believe what happened this afternoon. I've been with lots of girls, but I never saw them take off their clothes so freely. But, hey, I just went with the flow. It was fucking weird. I thought why would someone take us to the pond and go skinny-dipping? Why would a guy want us to see his girlfriend naked?"

Bobby had a whole different view on what had happened. "All I can see, man, when I close my eyes are her big bouncy bodacious breasts. They are the most beautiful breasts I have ever seen with those two brown rosettes just staring at me."

Barry had to agree. "I know, it was hard for me not to stare at them."

"Barry, you know how I like giving people nicknames? Well,

whenever I see her in my mind's eye, I think of her beautiful breasts and then I see her bushy mound, a thick carpet of black hair. I think I will call her the Bush-woman."

"Good night, Bobby."

"Good night, Barry."

"Hey, Bobby, do you really think they will come get us tomorrow?"

"I doubt it."

And true to Barry and Bobby's prediction, Johnny and his Lady Godiva, aka Bush-woman, never returned to get them.

Rising early, Barry and Bobby walked down the dirt road in the hopes of getting a ride. Chugging along and coming closer, they recognized the faded green VW with the hound dog a quarter mile away. They looked at each other.

"Oh shit, here they come," Bobby announced.

Barry shook his head. "There's no way in hell I am getting back into that car." They grabbed their packs, ran into the woods, lay on the ground until it was safe to venture back out on the road. Both agreed it was better to burn and blister than to get back into that hot cramped VW with that smelly dog.

More than a few hours of hitchhiking had passed to no avail as they walked in the blazing sun along Canada 1. Even with their best faces, appearing pleasant and nonthreatening, the few cars that did go by were not stopping. As they plodded along, they would switch thumbing duty on occasion, meaning the person on thumbing duty had to walk backward to face the oncoming traffic. Trudging along for miles, they found themselves approaching an area of vast cultivated fields. The expanse was tightly packed rows of thin green stalks topped with small bright yellow flowers called rapeseed. This plant they later learned was essential for making vegetable oil.

It was now Bobby's turn to walk backward. Facing the oncoming traffic, he saw that an old "Studebaker President, a big cushy road car, V8, with four doors and overstuffed seats" was slowing to a stop. The decision to stop and pick them up must have been determined when the occupants of the old "Studdy" first saw them at a distance. Most drivers wait until they have given hitchhikers a good looking over and usually drive past them before stopping. But the driver and passenger happened to be two bubbly and giddy eighteen-year-old girls.

They told the guys that they were locals. From the barrage of questions, they were also very curious about these offbeat boys in blue jeans thumbing through their hometown.

The passenger asked, "Where are you guys heading?"

Barry, with his usual charming smile, said, "We are going to Vancouver Island, and eventually, we want to go to San Francisco."

The passenger responded, "That is so cool!" Looking at her friend, she said, "We should plan a trip to San Francisco now that we have graduated from high school, Rachel."

Bobby, more intrigued by her car, asked Rachel, "Where did you get this fine car?"

"It was my grandfather's car. He gave it to me as a graduation present," she replied beaming.

The ride was short. Within forty-five minutes the girls were close to home. After the guys' expressions of gratitude for the ride and their heartfelt goodbyes, they were dropped off, out in the prairie lands.

Giggling, the girls yelled, "See you in San Francisco!"

Chapter 6

A NIGHT IN A HOSTEL AND A RODEO

THE PLAN FOR THE DAY was to reach the town of Medicine Hat, a small city located in the southeastern portion of Alberta, alongside the South Saskatchewan River. As with so many small towns, Canada 1 was now built around the city without having to pass through it. It was believed that years ago the highway passed through the center of the town; however, as the world increasingly traveled faster and farther by road, the inconvenience of passing through small, congested areas was eliminated with bypass highways. This elimination negatively impacted on the economy as potential consumers would not be stopping and spending their money.

From conversations with other travelers, Barry and Bobby learned their hostel was located on the highway—not in town. A person couldn't even see it from the highway. Their hope was to find their way to the hostel as soon as possible to secure a safe haven for the night. Road signs pointing the way were indications that they were nearing Medicine Hat. Off at a distance, on both sides of the road, people could be seen hitchhiking, further proving their goal was within reach. In the approximate center of these east- and westbound travelers, on the south side of the highway and separated by an easement and a wire fence, stood two large L-shaped portable buildings. People were milling about in the open area where the buildings intersected.

"This must be the place," Bobby said to the driver, "and probably the only reason why anybody would congregate out here in the middle of nowhere."

Their driver slowed.

Barry said, "This has to be it. Yeah, you can let us out here."

The driver pulled over and stopped. Once again, Barry and Bobby gathered up their backpacks. As they stepped out of the car, the eyes of a half dozen or more westbound hitchhikers were watching in the hopes that the driver would invite one of them to take their place.

"Thanks for the ride." The driver smiled, held up his hand in a final wave, pulled away, and disappeared. Crossing the highway, they stopped to talk with an eastbound traveler.

"This is the hostel, right?" asked Barry.

"Yup, check-in is right over there," he replied, pointing his index finger.

They nodded, thanked him, and walked through the gap in the fence to the common area where a few people sat at the picnic tables or stood talking. They walked through a small gathering, feeling somewhat invisible. Two or three of the guests raised their heads and nodded a cautious acknowledgement. Others, engaged in their conversation, were oblivious to their passing.

Both trudged through the coarse dark brown sand and through the common area to the point where the two buildings met. Hanging from the underside of a two-by-four-framed porch roof that ran along the front of both buildings was a sign that read Sign In. Under the sign, sitting on a stool behind a Dutch door, was a young man with long bushy red hair pulled back into a ponytail. He was, perhaps, in his mid-twenties. With a freckled face and penetrating blue eyes, similar to Barry's, he greeted them with a friendly, "Hi guys, where're you coming from?"

Together they gave him a brief explanation of where they had traveled from and how they were planning to eventually make their way to Vancouver Island.

"So, you guys are American, eh? You're lucky it's early. We still have some beds." He continued with a brief explanation, "If you're not familiar with the rules, they're pretty simple. It'll cost you $2.50 for a maximum of two days. If you can't pay the $2.50 you can earn your keep by helping out doing chores around here, designated by me. Picking up around the grounds, washing pots and pans, and doing general kitchen work or whatever else needs to be done. Quiet time is after ten. You are eligible for two meals a day, one in the morning and one in the evening. Breakfast is served at 6:00 and ends at 7:00. Dinner is from 5:00 to 6:00. We sure could use a little help around here so, if you want to volunteer for some work duties, I'd be much obliged." Gesturing with his hand, he said, "The showers are down there, as is the dormitory. Choose any bed that's not taken. Do you have any questions? If not, please sign your names on this sheet that shows you have read the rules. Welcome to Medicine Hat!"

"Thank you, it's great to be here," Barry replied sincerely.

"You can thank the Canadian government for making hostels available."

And with that, they walked off to find their beds, get settled, and shower off the sweat and caked-on street grit that had accumulated on their bodies from the previous day. It felt great to have showered and dressed in clean clothes. Who knew how long it would be before taking their next shower. Having only one change of clothes, these same clothes would be worn again the next day, and maybe the next day too. Socks and underwear could be washed in a sink when the opportunity presented itself.

Now it was time to join the others for the evening meal. The food, as well as the hostel circuit in general, was Canadian government surplus. The bread was of a very coarse texture, freshly baked on the premises. The loaves were round as opposed to a conventional loaf shape. The tins that served as baking pans were quart juice cans with the tops removed with a can opener. The bread was chewy but tasty. Neither one remembered what the main course was; it was something not worth remembering other than it was protein, and it filled the hole. Everyone always made it a point to consume everything that was laid out in front of them, unsure of when they would get their next meal.

Bobby had chosen to forgo the $2.50 fee and work, whereas Barry opted to pay. Bobby's duty that evening was to help in the kitchen by washing pots and pans, and he still believes to this day that he was the best pot-and-pan-man to ever grace the kitchen at the Medicine Hat hostel. Afterward, he joined Barry outside at the picnic tables to swap stories of the road with the other travelers. When they mentioned heading westbound en route to Vancouver Island, they were told that the hostel in Banff was a "must stop."

"Dude, you have to go to Banff. It's on the way. The incredible beauty of the place is far-out. It will blow your mind."

"Okay," Bobby assured him. "It's good to know. We'll have to check it out."

There was a peaceful air of camaraderie as the group exchanged stories and advice. Quiet time was now approaching, and a night of peaceful sleep in this sheltered setting felt good. It was a time to immerse themselves in the moment.

They awoke to the sounds of people beginning to bustle about, returning from the showers, getting dressed, talking softly, jostling their gear to their shoulders, clomping across the floor, down the steps, and finally out into the common area for coffee and breakfast.

Breakfast was surprisingly good. There was orange juice from concentrate, rather stout coffee, watery scrambled eggs, round bread toast, and a slab of government Spam with a slice of surplus cheese on top. Not bad. After notifying Mr. Red that they were leaving, Barry and Bobby walked through the opening in the fence and across the highway to the westbound side to take up their spot in the pecking order of the hitchhikers.

Barry and Bobby's next stop was Banff. Thumbing through Medicine Hat, they calculated that it was about 350 miles away. By pure luck, they didn't wait long. Coming down the road toward them, Bobby recognized a bronze, '65 Mercury Meteor. The driver slowed to take a look at them, and the car came to a stop. Barry's cardboard sign with the word **BANFF** in big, bold black letters must have caught his attention. They picked up their backpacks and hustled to the car. Looking at the sign, the man said, "Hey guys, I am heading to Jasper, and I can drop you off in Banff on my way through."

Barry immediately replied, "Hell, we don't even know where Jasper is, but if you can drop us off in Banff, that would be great."

The man, Dave, had a mild-natured demeanor, and it would be an understatement to say he was very skilled in conversation. He was in his mid-twenties, and he had graduated from the University of Calgary. The silver threads dispersed throughout his short black hair made him appear older. His story was he was heading home to Jasper where his parents owned a lodge. Dave was inquisitive and genuinely interested in their travels.

So, Barry began the chronicle of their trek across Canada beginning with, "We stepped onto a Peter Pan bus..." The conversation pivoted to their first failed trip, due in part to the inconsistent hitchhiking laws from state to state.

Big billboards advertising The Calgary Stampede Sixty-Year Jubilee loomed ubiquitously as the trio drew closer to Calgary.

Barry couldn't resist the temptation to ask, "What is this stampede all about? It seems like we're seeing signs every few miles."

Dave laughed. "You don't know about the Calgary Stampede? Man, you missed an extravaganza that just ended. You might even call it the 'Greatest Rodeo Show on Earth.' It started in 1912; hence the Sixty-Year Jubilee. The opening show starts with a grand old parade and lasts for ten days."

Bobby, chimed in, "I haven't heard of it until now. What are some of the events?"

"I would venture to say, the list of events is endless." Dave continued to spout a catalog of competitions, "There is steer wrestling, bull riding, barrel racing, chuck wagon racing, wild cow milking, wild horse racing, and saddle bronc bareback riding, just to name a few."

Not wanting to hear the specifics of each and every event, Barry asked, "Do you have a favorite?"

"It's hard to say because I like them all, but the first competition that comes to mind is the wild cow-milking stampede. Yes, you heard me right, the wild cow-milking competition. Now, these old cows have never set foot in a barn, and they don't like being corralled, so they are as ornery as hell! You can imagine what happens when they are set loose. So, what you have is a working duo. The first cowboy is the roper who moves fast and furiously to lasso the feral cow. Once the cow is secured, the second cowboy, the milker, grabs and squeezes those big old udders over the mouth of a glass bottle. The fastest cowboy carrying the most milk in the bottle wins the competition." (The wild cow-milking and the wild horse race competitions are no longer part of the rodeo show.)

There was a polite chuckle, more from confusion than amusement since neither of them knew Canada was such a big cattle country.

"On a more serious note, I have to say the saddle bronc bareback riding competition is one of the most thrilling events. Watching a cowboy try to keep himself on that horse for eight seconds can be a nail-biting experience."

Curious, Barry asked, "Do you go every year? It sounds like a good time, but I don't think I could spend days watching rodeo shows."

"I haven't been since I was a teenager. In addition to the Stampede, there's square-dancing and continuous music of the western bands for entertainment."

Barry and Dave conversed about how the stampede put Calgary on the map for the duration of the ride. Dave learned about the States, and the guys learned more than they cared to know about the Calgary Stampede.

While they were passing through Calgary and were heading toward Banff, a small town in Alberta, it became apparent that they were getting closer to the Canadian Rockies. From the front seat, Barry could see the approaching foothills and the jagged, pointed peaks of the mountain range. Barry and Bobby had never seen mountains so breathtakingly beautiful. The closer they got the more majestic their panoramic view became. New England's mountains paled in comparison. They were now transitioning from the Calgary prairie grasslands to the Canadian Rocky foothills. The old '65 Merc was now committed to climbing in elevation up the steep winding mountain highway. At the top stood the jewel of the Canadian Rockies, Banff National Park. The awe-inspiring ride to Banff finally came to an end, so they picked up their backpacks, thanked Dave, and walked toward their hostel.

Chapter 7

THE SOUTH SIDE OF THE TRANS-CANADA HIGHWAY

ON THE SOUTH SIDE OF the Trans-Canada Highway, nestled in the tall timber of the ancient mountain forest, stood the Banff Youth Hostel settlement where they planned to spend the night. This particular hostel was made up of an array of big white military tents. Their tent was a canvas structure, and inside the tent, there were cloth drapes that formed a barrier to keep in the heat. In the American army, it would have been called the GP large, a General Purpose large (eighteen feet by fifty-two feet) tent. Wooden-framed cots occupied the center aisle.

Barry and Bobby were fortunate to get cots against the wall, which shielded them from the continuous buzz about the grizzly bear that had been seen scouting outside the tent the night before. The warning was clear: do not venture out after dark; a hungry bear may still be lurking in the woods.

After a restless sleep, both had the same thought, What the hell, let's get up and head for the hot springs. And despite the chance encounter with a bear, they got up quietly just before sunrise. They walked along the well-trodden path, a rocky trail through the forest. Traveling through veils of heavy mist, they heard the sound of footsteps and caught a glimpse of ethereal shapes of visitors coming toward them as they made their way down the mountain.

The water from the springs was so warm, and the air so cold, that a dome of fog formed over the stream that flowed all the way down to the hostel. Clothing, towels, and shoes were carefully placed to ensure their dryness. At the pool, Barry and Bobby stripped down to their white BVDs and eased themselves into the water. A good fifteen minutes was all that was necessary to satisfy their curiosity. Back at the hostel, they sat down and dug into the eggs, Spam, and day-old bread, and gulped down the weak coffee. Afterward, they packed for their next destination—Vancouver Island!

There was a shift in consciousness. Their worlds were expanding and for the first time their small New England cosmos fell away. Their experiences became more than just a ride from one hostel to another. Now they were immersed in the stunning sensory splendor on every side and even beyond their present scope of life.

Barry and Bobby walked perhaps a mile from the hostel to start a fresh segment of the Trans-Canada Highway. Once again, they stood on the side of the highway with their thumbs out. In a short time, a car stopped. They loaded up in a nondescript vehicle and were on their way. The driver was heading to Kamloops, about six hours from where they stood.

During the ride, Barry mentioned how he wanted to see Lake Louise and would regret not seeing it since they were so close to it. (Lake Louise was named after Princess Louise, daughter of Queen Victoria.)

Barry was surprised when the driver said it was well worth seeing, and since he was in no hurry would be happy to oblige. The forty-minute drive to Lake Louise was spectacular! In Bobby's words:

The highway leading west out of the mountains was draped with sheer cliffs covered in glacial ice. Even in the early summer warmth of mid-July, the ice covering the mountains was tens of feet thick. Melted ice flowed down forming in rivulets. The water was relentless in its cascade as it fell into the swales that men had engineered to capture and direct the water to their will. There were still sheets of ice, tens of feet thick, hanging from the cliff. We passed through avalanche sheds, wooden tunnel-like structures with sloping roofs, built over the roads to protect the highway from avalanches.

Since the fury of winter had passed, and the relative warmth of spring and summer had arrived, the ice pack had diminished to a substantial degree. This was evidenced by a sea of thirty-foot-huge trunks of fir trees whose length from that point upward had been snapped off in the violence of avalanches. The remains of the treetops lay in a tangled, twisted mess, hundreds of feet below the road. Perhaps thirty feet of ice had melted away at this point, creating the headwaters of great rivers.

The trip to Lake Louise on the Bow River did not disappoint. And although they never stepped out of the car, they witnessed a majestic view. Barry found the translucent blue-green hues of Lake Louise breathtaking. The alpine glacier, which formed Lake Louise from its melting glacial debris, was aptly named Victoria in 1897. And she alone continues to be the exquisite imperial backdrop of Lake Louise. Positioned on each side of Victoria's imposing structure emerged the towering snowcapped mountains. Surrounding the lake like sentinels, stood lofty spruce, pine, and fir trees.

Back on Canada 1 the image of Lake Louise with all its splendor lingered in their minds. While Bobby sat quietly in the backseat of the car, he made a sudden and important discovery—a discovery that would change the trajectory of their trip. On the overpass,

Bobby noticed that there was a train running on the tracks below them. Beyond the overpass, the highway now ran parallel to the train tracks. "Hey, Barry, you see what I see?"

The pace was easy, the ride smooth as they descended the foothills and entered the high prairie town of Kamloops. The town consisted of a strip of businesses on each side of the highway complete with gas stations, an abandoned motel, and a lone diner. It was now late afternoon, and Barry and Bobby were grateful to have made it safely from Banff to Kamloops.

The driver stopped in front of a Pullman-style diner, saying, "This is a good place to drop you guys off."

They thanked him, wished him well, and said goodbye before entering the diner.

Sitting down at the counter, they perused the menu. Barry and Bobby knew they had to be frugal, but they also knew they could order more than "a toothpick and a glass of water." (Hat tipped to a native son, Dan Aykroyd.) There were two young girls, pretty girls—a blue-eyed blonde and a blue-eyed brunette—sitting at the counter a few seats down from where they were. The girls were probably eighteen or nineteen. The foursome tried to avert their lingering glances but without success. The mutual attraction was unmistakable.

Finally, the unspoken magnetism was broken when the brunette started the conversation, "Where are you guys from? We've never seen you here before."

Bobby seized the moment to connect. "We started out from Massachusetts, U.S.A. We are on our way to Vancouver Island."

"Oh, you guys are from the United States? You guys are a long way from Massachusetts."

Barry added, "We're hitchhiking across Canada, then down through California. We want to swing through San Francisco, and maybe even the Haight-Ashbury district, where all the hippies and musicians like the Grateful Dead hang out. We may even go as far as Mexico."

The blonde, who had been silent blurted out, "Wow, California! Cool. So, what are ya guys up to tonight?"

Barry shrugged his shoulders before he spoke, "Not sure yet. But all we know is that we need to find a place to crash for the night."

The blonde looked at Barry. "I have an idea. And by the way, I'm Jennifer," and pointing to the brunette added, "She's Lizzy."

"I'm Barry. This is my buddy, Bobby."

Jennifer continued, "Not too far from here is an abandoned motel. If you guys have your sleeping bags and everything, you might want to crash there."

Bobby looked at Barry. "OK, let's go check it out."

Barry and Bobby followed the girls out of the diner. They noticed the girls were dressed similar to the girls back home—indigo blue bell-bottoms, T-shirts, and large hoop earrings. This was one of the few occasions where there was no rivalry. Barry was drawn to the blonde and Bobby liked the brunette. As they walked, the girls explained that the motel was a clandestine meeting place where teen townies came together to drink and party.

Approaching the rundown area with no trees or greenery and ramshackle houses, they came to a long desolate motel nearly obscured by waist-high grass and overgrown shrubs. Set back from the highway the motel was not only neglected but trashed. The place had been vandalized and long stripped of anything valuable. Windows were smashed, doors had been removed, the interior block walls were pocked with holes, and mounds of rubble littered the floors. Beer and wine bottles, many reduced to shards of glass, were strewn about. The graffiti on the walls was further evidence of raucous gatherings. The strong odor of urine permeated the air.

They scrutinized their surroundings, looked at the girls, and exchanged glances. Barry and Bobby instinctively and unilaterally arrived at the same conclusion: the place was a dump, and no doubt a biohazard, and it was crazy to consider rolling out there for the night. But the girls were so pretty and the vibes they were sending out were as alluring as a siren's song.

However, as the girls continued to describe the parties and the usual shenanigans of teenaged townies, sane thoughts began to emerge along with overpowering hints of apprehension.

Barry's immediate thoughts were, *There is no way I can sleep in this funky, smelly place with shit all over the place. I just want to get some sleep in a secluded place with no hassles. I don't want to end up dead in Kamloops.*

Bobby's thoughts were more on the edgy side. "All I could think of was the underaged and hormonal teens, illegal drinking, possible drugs, territorial brawling, maybe even ending up in fisti-cuffs. Even worse, Barry and I, being strangers in town, could even bring the attention of the police. It was just too risky."

They rebounded back to reality just in time to hear, "So, you guys want to hang out and sleep here tonight?"

Stillness, seconds that felt like minutes passed, while they searched for a polite way to reject their offer.

The girls smiled and waited expectantly.

Finally, Barry broke the silence. "Sorry, as much as we would like to hang out with you girls, it's been a really long day, and we need to be on the road by daylight."

Disappointment, almost palpable, was so clearly written on the girls' faces. And in truth, the guys were disappointed too. There would be no good times that night. But after weighing the risks, their common sense tipped the scales against any thoughts of stay-ing. Under different circumstances maybe things could have ended differently.

They all walked back to the diner where everything started. Lizzy said, "See you guys later."

Jennifer grinned. "I hope you make it to California. Have a safe trip."

Chapter 8

FORTUITOUS MEETING
OF THE TWO IRISHMEN

AFTER LEAVING THE DINER FOR a second time that day, the guys took up their practiced vigil with their thumbs out to the oncoming traffic. A gas station was directly across the highway from where they stood. Two men were standing alongside a new '72 Ford Galaxie 500XL, while an attendant filled the fuel tank, raised the hood, and checked the fluids. One of the men looked over to Barry and Bobby and began to shout, motioning for them to come to the other side of the road to where he was. Curious, they crossed the street to see what this man wanted. On closer inspection, wearing his Izod shirt, dressed in black slacks, and shiny loafers, he looked to be a well-to-do gentleman with discerning taste.

"Do you have a license to drive?"

"Yes."

"Where are you guys headed?"

"Vancouver Island," replied Barry.

"Perfect! OK, here's the deal." Gesturing toward his car where his business partner was sitting in the passenger seat, he continued, "If you drive us to Vancouver City, about 250 miles from here, and get us there by early morning I'll buy your ferry tickets to Vancouver Island."

They both looked at each other in disbelief, then looked at the man and said, "Hell, yeah!" To Barry it was a no-brainer. What might have taken them two days of travel was only a twenty-four-hour trip. But for Bobby, this was a dream come true! "What could be better than driving a new top of the line '72 and a half, fastback Ford Galaxie XL with a 428 Cobra Jet V8? There wasn't a man in the world who wouldn't want to get his hands on a ride of this caliber!"

They got into the back seat. Barry rode shotgun and Bobby was at the wheel. "The interior was rolled and pleated, burgundy leather. Front buckets with a console, mounted tach and gear shift lever. This beast could swallow continents at a hundred miles per hour all day long." So here he was in the driver's seat with this fine car at his fingertips, pointed down 250 miles of open road. Bobby adjusted the seat and mirrors and then asked, "Is everybody ready?" And with that Bobby wheeled the big Ford out of the gas station and out onto the highway.

The two men were Canadians in their late forties, but surprisingly, spoke with an Irish brogue. They were businessmen. The owner of the car introduced himself as Patrick. His companion, Michael, came along for the ride and the opportunity to meet Patrick's sister in Vancouver City where they planned to spend the night.

Michael, a portly ruddy-skinned fellow with a thick head of red hair and a beard to match, broke out a bottle of Rock and Rye whiskey, which they passed back and forth. Before long, they were singing Irish lullabies (no joke) at the top of their voices and having a grand old time laughing, stomping their feet, and slapping their knees in time. Barry dozed off, but Bobby with white knuckles on the wheel, was rocketing down the highway, just "digging the shit out of this fine car." Hours later, the singing had stopped; the revelers had passed out. Bobby began to pick up speed and barreled through the region of Fraser Canyon. The road, straight and un-bending for miles and miles, was a perfect playground for Bobby. The reflectors embedded in the roadway, illuminated by the head-lights, seemed to go into infinity. He was cruising at about a hun-dred miles an hour. Effortlessly and smoothly, the big Ford sliced through the cool night air.

Off in the distance, perhaps a mile or so, Bobby saw the red glow of taillights. He now had a target. He vividly recalled, "I wick-ed up speed to close the distance, but my target was proving to be difficult to catch. I could see that I was slowly gaining, and finally, I was a couple of car lengths behind my quarry. I pushed the pedal to the floor, and instantly, the big Ford shifted down into passing gear as the needle on the tachometer jerked to the red line. I shifted back up into high gear and was standing on the pedal as I shot past. I saw the car's bright yellow paint with the black bumblebee stripe wrapped around the tail, and I recognized what it was. This was not your garden-variety Dodge. This was a Super Bee!"

Super Bees were powered with a high performance 383 Wedge with a 750 CFM Holley, mated to a 727 Torqueflite automatic, or in more rare versions, a four-speed manual.

"I scanned the mirror looking for my opponent, expecting to see the Dodge far behind. After all, I was driving a 428 Cobra Jet. In my mind, I should have been far ahead. Even at this speed, I could hear the bellow of a fully open four-barrel coming closer, pulling up alongside me and blowing right on by! The Dodge pulled for about three hundred feet, and as it throttled back, I saw blue flames shooting out of the two exhaust tips. I stood on the pedal once again to close the distance. The driver of the Dodge saw me coming and accelerated. I managed to pull up door handle to door handle before the surging Dodge once again pulled away.

"It was clear that the Dodge was the faster car. There was no need to continue the contest. At this point, I was content to ride behind the Dodge. This was the fastest that I had ever driven in my life. I was buzzing with buck fever and was glad to be finished!"

In the back seat, Michael was now awake and perched on his elbows between the front seats looking forward. He was quite alert considering how whiskeyed-up he was a few hours earlier. "Ah...you know, the cops patrol this stretch of road pretty heavy. You might want to slow down."

"Yeah, you're right, I should slow down."

The contest was over, and the Dodge and the Ford were content to travel together, one behind the other, at a safer speed. Nearing an off-ramp, the Dodge turned on the right turn signal and slowed to exit. As they passed the decelerating Dodge, the driver's window went down to reveal the face of a woman!

Bobby, humbled, nodded in respect.

It was after midnight, and they were nearing Vancouver City. Patrick had to be roused from his sleep so he could guide Bobby through the city streets to his sister's apartment. They pulled up curbside in front of a turn-of-the-century redbrick storefront in a neighborhood of similar structures. She lived in an apartment on the second floor, accessible by a flight of steel stairs that ran up alongside the building from an alley that was perpendicular to the main street. The staircase was probably a fire escape in an earlier life. A light hung over the door at the top of the stairs, and they ascended single file. He knocked on the door. Through the window a light turned on and soft footsteps approached the door, a voice said, "Who is it?"

"It's me," said Patrick.

The dead bolt clacked, and the door swung open. Standing in the doorway was a tall, thin woman in her late thirties. Other than the tangle of brown hair framing her face and casting a shadow on her sleepy eyes, her appearance was neat and well-kept. She clutched her bathrobe with one hand, as she ushered them in with the other. Patrick affectionately greeted his sister with a hug. Michael, followed by Barry and Bobby, was introduced to Meghan. Greetings over, Patrick explained how Barry and Bobby had been added to the group; then he excused himself and shuffled off to a waiting bed. He needed to get his rest to sleep off the rest of the whiskey. He had an important day ahead and wanted to be fresh and clear-thinking.

The remaining four stayed up talking. She offered them some beer and after a while broke out some pot. If Michael had any hopes of spending some alone time getting to know Meghan, that notion was fading; he staggered to the couch, lay down, and fell asleep.

Now Meghan, Barry, and Bobby continued their conversation. They found her lighthearted and engaging. Barry and Bobby sat on the living room floor around her coffee table, getting high and enjoying her company. They spoke in hushed tones so as not to wake up the others. To keep the party going, Barry and Bobby had to make a hasty beer run. It wasn't a problem; bars didn't close until 2:00 a.m. They put their shoes back on and walked to one of the local bars to get some beer. After they returned, they continued to drink more beers. Barry rolled another joint and passed it to Meghan. Between a few coughs and some seeds popping, the three talked for another hour about politics and how they got to where they were at this point in their travels. The chatter went on well into the wee hours of the morning until sleep became a necessity. Before the guys crashed on the carpeted hardwood living room floor, Bobby motioned to the couch where Michael lay sleeping. Bobby joked, "I hope we didn't intrude."

She rolled her eyes and said, "It's cool. Hey, it was fun getting to hang out with you guys."

~~~

Bobby was roused by the smell of coffee and the clanking of coffee mugs. Barry was still sound asleep.

Patrick yelled, "Time to get up guys; we have to catch the morning ferry."

Meghan and Michael both got up to see them off.

Patrick said, "Maybe you can show Michael around the city. I'll be back tomorrow."

Patrick now took the wheel as they pulled away from the curb and headed for the ferry port. Drawing closer, they saw the ferry was already at the dock, and there were already lines of cars waiting to embark in the staging area. While waiting to board the ship, they could see a ticket man walking between the rows of cars collecting fares. Patrick once again thanked them for getting him and his business partner to where they needed to be, on time, and all in one piece. And true to his word, he paid the fare to Vancouver Island as a token of his appreciation.

The ramp was finally lowered, and the waiting hoard of cars and passengers began to file into the bowels of the ship. Deckhands motioned instructions to the drivers to come forward and to stop: motors off, emergency brakes on, and car in park. Once the car was secured, they were free to roam about the boat. The seasoned passengers stayed in their cars, drinking coffee, reading the morning paper, or napping. But for Barry and Bobby, being on a big ship was a new endeavor. They wanted to take in and savor the whole experience.

The three of them walked up the stairs to the observation deck where, if you chose to, you could sit in what resembled a departure area at an airport. There were rows of seats that faced forward so that the passengers could look out through the cabin windows at the scenery passing by. There were kiosks that sold food items, magazines, and newspapers. They walked through the center aisle of the boat to the rear and out through the doors into the fresh air of the stern deck.

The view was beyond incredible. As they sailed away from Vancouver City, white-tipped Mount Rainier and the Cascade Mountains to the south were in full view. And front and south, were the majestic, snowcapped Olympic Mountains. The ocean was a beautiful navy blue, accented by the white froth of the prop wash in the wake of the ship. The voyage took less than two hours.

As the ship neared the port of Nanaimo, Vancouver Island, the captain announced over the P.A. that people should begin to return to their cars in preparation to disembark. Their time with Patrick was coming to an end. It was agreed that Barry and Bobby would once again be on their own when they arrived on the Island.

Before their final departure, Patrick asked, "Hey, do you fellas like oysters?"

Barry had never had oysters before and was indifferent. Barry was an Ipswich clam man; he liked them steamed, deep-fried, and whole belly.

Since Bobby had been taught to eat oysters at an early age, he was quick to respond, "Heck yeah! I grew up on 'em!"

"Well...I'll drop you guys off at a beach where you can gather and eat oysters to your hearts' content," he said, gesturing toward the water. After a short drive from the ferry, Patrick pulled over to the curb and pointed to a wooden staircase that led down to the beach about fifty feet down the cliff. He popped the trunk so the guys could retrieve their backpacks. They shook hands with mutual respect and gratitude, well wishes exchanged, and he drove away.

Anticipating a gourmet meal of fresh raw oysters on the half shell, they descended the stairs to the rock-strewn pebble beach below. Patrick was right. From the low tide level on out into the bay, the water was littered with oysters. Barry gathered and struggled to open them with his dull pointed scout knife, but never having opened an oyster before, and not having the appropriate tool, he couldn't get the proper angle or entry point to sever the muscle that held the shell's halves. Consequently, the tip of the blade slipped off the shell and stuck itself about a quarter of an inch into his forearm. "Shit!!" He examined his cut, poking and squeezing it. The blood trickled and droplets fell to the ground.

Bobby surveyed the damage. "Meh...not too bad." With that said, Bobby continued to open an oyster. "Ah...oyster on the half shell!" He raised it to his mouth and slid it in. The taste, contrary to what he had expected, was awful! Upon close examination, the oyster was awash in a milky goo that tasted nasty, probably akin to the taste of rotten meat. The only explanation Bobby could come up with was that maybe it was mating season, and this milky goo was... well, you know. That pretty much ended their oyster escapade. "Oh well." They headed back up the stairs to the road. The plan was to navigate their way to the hostel in Nanaimo for a meal, a shower, a bed, and a good night's sleep.

Chapter 9

NANAIMO

THE LONG STAIRCASE LEADING UP from the pebbled beach ended at the edge of the road. With a long sigh, suggesting the end of one journey and the anticipation of another, they set their packs down to determine exactly where they were. Just as they were getting ready to stick out their thumbs, they spotted a little four-seater, '70 Mercury Capri sports car with four girls in it. The car slowed to take a look at them with four pairs of eyes fixated on the two long-haired handsome young men standing on the side of the road. The car came to an abrupt stop about fifty feet beyond them. One of the girls popped up through the sunroof, looked at them, and bent back down into the car for a quick parley. She reemerged.

"Do you guys need a ride?

Bobby said, "Yeah.

"Come on. Where are you going?"

"We are hoping to make it to the hostel in Nanaimo," he answered. "Do you know where it is?"

Sunroof girl replied, "We sure do. It's about a ten- or fifteen-minute ride from Oyster Beach. Squeeze in."

Squeezing in this small car with only four seat placements was an understatement, but somehow, the guys figured out a way to compress their bodies and backpacks into the car with them. The fact that the arrangement required two of the girls having to sit on their laps was fine with them. Bobby's first thought was, *Oh yes, please.*

The talk was all about the guys. The girls were intrigued with their Northeastern American manner of speaking, their accent pleasing. For the duration of the ride, they were giggly, bouncy, and fun. As they pulled up to the curb in front of the hostel, Barry said, "We desperately need to find a laundromat. Can you tell us where the nearest one is?" One girl said that there was a local one in the center of town. Barry and Bobby got out of the car, thanked them, and smiled. Something undefined and unspoken hung in the air as all stood looking at each other. Thoughts and words became tangled leaving only silence. Then the car pulled away, hands waving through the sunroof and out the windows.

As one might guess, their brief encounter was not over. They would all meet again, and they would all have the opportunity to tell their own stories in a short space of time. And Barry and Bobby, who were in their sexual prime and looking for more than just friendship at the time, got more than what they had sought.

They learned firsthand about the plague of poverty, experienced the magnificent beauty of Maple Bay, and were awakened to a whole new culture—the Coast Salish Indians. Even to this day, more than fifty years later, recollections of Mae, Ana, Erin, and Helen have not faded.

Barry and Bobby went up the staircase and into the hostel. They were happy for the ride and the brief company of these lively, vibrant young women. The building that housed the hostel might have once been a church. It was of broken block concrete construction, painted white. It wasn't a large building, maybe fifty feet wide and seventy-five feet deep. It was two-storied with a basement. The floors were crunchy, squeaky hardwood. The entrance door was situated in the center of a foyer with a staircase running left and right down to the sidewalk. The sidewalk to the right of the building angled downhill alongside the small city street toward the bay at the bottom of the hill and the waterfront commerce area. Barry and Bobby checked in with the person manning the desk and were given an area with cots to sleep on. The shower room was in the basement.

After showering, they went back to the dormitory area, sat on their cots, and struck up conversations with some of the other travelers. They learned that there was a big "to-do." The event was the Nanaimo Bathtub Races. It was an international event that had begun a few years earlier, and every year hence, had grown in popularity. This year's competition was forecast to be the biggest yet. The talk and excitement steadily gaining momentum had piqued their interest. They definitely wanted to check it out!

The carnival atmosphere of the Bathtub Races lived up to the hype. Bayside, downtown Nanaimo was bustling with spectators and participants. The public parking lots, transformed into the pit area, were jammed with tow vehicles and trailers upon which the bathtubs were transported. Pit crews were tuning and tweaking their creations in preparation for the long-anticipated race. Prospective racers were zipping their boats around in the water, testing and practicing the course. The public was welcome to wander through the pits as the crews prepared their entries.

The bathtubs weren't really bathtubs. Most were fabricated out of fiberglass or Styrofoam. For example, one boat was concocted out of cardboard milk cartons, which broke apart in the test phase. The two-man crew were hamming it up as the pieces floated away, leaving them flailing away in an exaggerated manner, much to the delight of the crowd. Mostly, the boats were hydrofoils with a faux bathtub perched on top, powered by a small outboard motor. The crews would don various costumes to enhance the jovial atmosphere. Some wore bathrobes and shower caps, fuzzy house slippers, curlers in their hair, clown hair, face paint, and the works. One boat had showerheads arranged that squirted water on the pilot as he raced.

Many of these makeshift boats were not very seaworthy, which added to the fun, in that they handled badly and would be easily swamped in the wake of other boats. For the most part, serious competition was not the object for most of the competitors. The object was to have fun, to enhance the party atmosphere, and to participate in the excitement. However, there were some boats that were engineered with great skill and much thought. These were the boats that would survive their race heats and be grouped together at the end of the race day for the finale.

The racing teams in the pit area would display the flag of their native countries. Even New Zealand and Australia were represented. Differing languages and accents could be heard spoken in the crowds. There were beer and food vendors lining the street. As the day wore on, the crowd collectively became intoxicated. Inhibitions were diminishing as the crowd melded into one happy party. Camaraderie was the order of the day. Neither Barry nor Bobby ever heard a harsh word or witnessed any belligerence the whole time. International goodwill prevailed.

As the day wound down, the activities bayside began to shift toward the bars. Barry and Bobby were swept along and into a large under-roof area where hundreds of people had already gathered to continue the party. This place was the Tally Ho, a convention hall associated with the hotel that shared its name. Round-top tables and chairs were filled to capacity. The music was loud, as were the shouts. In perfect tempo, the waitresses wended their way through the crowd delivering pitchers of beer to the revelers at the tables.

As they sat drinking their beers, making small talk with their neighbors, the crowd at the far end of the room erupted in full-throated cheers that went on for some time. People were now standing and craning their necks to see what the commotion was all about. The doors at the far end of the hall were opened and a guy on a chopper made his way into the hall, revving the engine and laughing all the way. People stood, some on the tabletops, and hoisted their beers, cheering him on. Tables and chairs had to be moved out of the way for the bike to pass through.

The crowd willingly cooperated in shuffling around the furniture to accommodate the cyclist's passage. He was met with adulation and pats on the back. Many were in disbelief that such a raucous thing was in fact happening, including Barry and Bobby. The biker made it through to the center of the room and exited out the main entrance with outraged management hanging on his shoulder, gnashing their teeth, and frantically shouting into his ears. Probably some civil codes were broken. The buzz about the bike continued on for some time.

The next event was "the shower of beer." It started slowly over on the opposite side of the room and eventually spread to the whole place. Glasses of beer were being emptied into the air that rained down on the crowd below. Everybody was loving it. Barry and Bobby hunkered down, hoping that they wouldn't be hit. Bobby tells this story best:

As we sat there looking at each other, a full twelve ounces of beer hit me in the back of my neck and ran down my back and into my pants. It came from the next table to our rear. I was not happy. Our attire was meager and now these clothes would need to be cleaned before they could be worn again or stored away in the backpack. I method-

ically filled my beer glass with a gathering malice, turned to meet the eye of my assailant, and let him have it, right in the face. I waited for his reaction. I was prepared for come what may. I could have gotten my ass kicked. I didn't care. He sat there wide-eyed and totally surprised, tense and dripping, and only offered up 'Oh, how nonchalant.' That was it. Thank God.

The beer showering was getting out of hand. Geysers of beer were erupting everywhere now. It was at the height of this that management decided to announce that the throwing of beer had to stop or beer sales would be curtailed. The announcement fell on deaf ears. The crowd was having too much fun. Moments later the house lights came on, the music stopped abruptly, and an announcement was made that the party was over and for everyone to exit the building. This was met with a chorus of boos. But the happy crowd willingly exited the building.

It was late. After a night of underage drinking and having been drenched with beer, they retreated to the hostel and showered, each taking turns wary of unsuspecting takers. Barry fell victim to losing five dollars, but he was grateful it wasn't his whole wallet. The next morning, they sought out a laundromat to wash their clothes of suds, sweat, and beers. All of their stuff needed to be washed. Being at the laundromat reminded Bobby of the movie Midnight Cowboy where the main character only had the clothes on his back, and when he went to the laundry, he stuffed his things into a running washer full of someone else's clothes, snatched them out before they were finished, and loaded them into a dryer of yet another person, all the while trying to conceal himself with a newspaper, while wearing only his underpants.

They weren't that bad off. They were wearing clothes. They batched their clothes together as one wash wearing only their pants and shirts. Having carefully folded and loaded their things into their backpacks, Mae came rushing into the laundromat and shouted, "I knew we would find you here! What are your plans for the day?"

"We really don't have anything planned. We just finished doing our laundry. What are you up to?" asked Barry.

The threesome walked out of the laundromat and over to the '70 Mercury Capri. Ana popped her head out of the roof, smiling broadly and obviously happy to see them again. "It's been a while."

Mae didn't lose a moment. "Hey guys, we were just riding around and thought you might need a place to stay. I'm house-sitting for my brother while he is away in the States on business. We girls have the place for the week. If you're interested, why don't you come and hang out with us."

Bingo! This might have been what was left hanging in the air, unsaid, when they parted the day before. Barry and Bobby weren't going to let the opportunity pass again. Without consulting with each other and with a fleeting glance, they both voiced, "Cool!" So once again, girls and guys loaded up into the small car and drove off.

All of the young women were college friends off for the summer. Mae, who immediately came across as the Alpha female, was a native Nanaimo Indian. She was short, solidly built and wore her long straight jet-black hair in two thick braids. Ana was also a Nanaimo Indian, but she was somewhat of an anomaly. Her fair skin, kinky whitish blond hair, pale hazel eyes might have led people to think she was an albino. She was about five-foot-six, slender, and extremely toned. Erin appeared to be of Irish descent, and to Barry and Bobby, she was beautiful. She had wavy dirty blond hair, ice-blue eyes, and a peaches-and-cream complexion with a few freckles thrown in. Like Ana, her body was toned and fit. Helen, a generously proportioned Caucasian girl, was rather reserved. She didn't reveal much of herself during the ride or during subsequent meetings. She presented herself with an air of suspicion the whole time and remained standoffish.

Mae's brother's house was a short distance down the road from Nanaimo in the town of Duncan. Here, as was the case on most of the Island, the land sloped down to the ocean. Her brother's house was an upscale deckhouse built on the side of the slope, falling away to the sea below. It was a couple of tiers up the hill from other homes below in a very nice locale with a beautiful view of the extended bay. Mae offered them the television room downstairs since the girls were planning to sleep in the rooms upstairs on the main floor.

They sat around the kitchen table. While eating lunch they shared bits and pieces of their lives. Helen was still aloof, but Erin slowly emerged from her shell of shyness and became much more animated. She spoke proudly about her dad, a doctor, and she hoped to follow in his footsteps. Unlike Ana and Mae, she appeared more complex and less self-absorbed. There was an air of sophistication, of introspection that drew Barry's attention to her from their first encounter. Their furtive glances back and forth and subtle warm smiles—when they thought no one was looking—indicated the attraction was mutual.

Ana and Mae were swimming instructors. They had a scheduled route through the reservations to teach the young kids how to swim and would be doing their route that afternoon. They invited the guys to come along with them. They eagerly accepted, knowing it was an unexpected gift to learn about and witness the lives of the Native Nanaimo Indians.

The three different locations that they went to were all along the Nanaimo River. The kids, aged from about five to ten years old, were there and waiting for the girls. Ana and Mae were very structured and disciplined in their approach to the lessons. This was serious stuff that they were teaching. The Nanaimo River was about fifty feet across and had a swift-moving current. It meandered its way from the highlands of the Island, snaked, making its way through the reservations, and finally to the estuary to the sea. The water attracted the young people, and on occasion would claim one of them. The girls felt it was their personal duty to prevent unnecessary drowning, a noble gesture, since they received no money.

Apart from the lessons, about a hundred feet upstream there was a railroad trestle, where the older kids would climb up on and jump into the river below. Although it was not very high, perhaps twenty feet or so, it posed a great danger. The menace lay in the fierce raging current below and the grueling swim to shore. While the lesson was going on, Barry and Bobby decided to go in for a swim. The water was cold, really cold. Barry dove in first and found himself immediately in deep water right off the bank.

The whirlpool of the current captured him and swept him to the bottom of the river, where an exerting downward force was holding him pinned deep. Being a strong swimmer, he had the inner fortitude and swimming expertise to push off the bottom with his feet to break through the hold that the river had on him. He surfaced, thankful to be alive. After viewing Barry's ordeal, Bobby thought it best to forgo the plunge. Ana and Mae were all too aware of that danger when Barry related his experience. They all traveled a couple of miles to the next location and then to the next where the girls would once again use their patience, strength, and skill to teach the young swimmers.

That evening, after a full day of sun and swimming with the girls, they returned to Mae's brother's house. The girls wanted to show the guys a good time and suggested that they go to a nightclub called the Maple Bay Casino. There was a lively crowd, music, pool tables, and beer. It sounded as though it would be a fun night and they agreed to go. But first Mae needed to contact someone. Mae took the driver's seat while her friend Ana sat in the passenger seat. Barry and Bobby sat in the back seat.

The first stop was a bar frequented by Native Indians only. Barry and Bobby were eyed suspiciously by the crowd, but they felt safe being in the presence of Ana and Mae. Considering the history, their animosity against white people was understandable. Mae had been given a tip that the person she was seeking might be at home on the reservation. The feeling of relief when Barry and Bobby left the bar was supplanted by uneasiness as they rode through the reservation.

Seeing firsthand the deplorable human conditions on the reservation flooded them first with shock, then sadness. Situated on a grid of quarter-acre lots, the small, square block houses might have had about seven hundred square feet of living space. Gravel roads were parallel and perpendicular to one another. The telltale signs of abject poverty were everywhere. Open windows with tattered curtains were blowing in the breeze. Front doors wide open. Junk washing machines, cars, and children's plastic toys littered the yards.

It was difficult to believe that people actually lived in these dwellings, but they did. Mae said that for most of the year, the Indians were on the government dole. However, during spawning season, the men would mobilize and feverishly fish for salmon, which brought in much needed money. The rest of the year, many succumbed to drinking. Mae never did find the person she was looking for.

~~~

The Maple Bay Casino, an upscale nightclub, was perched upon a cliff facing Maple Bay. The asphalt parking lot had a fresh coat of sealer on it. The exterior of the building was covered in a fresh coat of rustic red paint over what seemed to be cedar clapboards. Large sparkling windows overlooked the parking lot and, more importantly, Maple Bay and out to the sea. There was a canopy over the walkway that led from the parking lot to the front door. The club was tastefully furnished and inviting.

There was perhaps a half dozen tavern-type pool tables with Tiffany lampshades overhead illuminating them. In addition to plenty of tables and chairs, there was a bar aligned with stools. Music played over a quality sound system. Upon arriving the parking lot was already nearly full. The club was bustling with young people drinking, socializing, and playing pool. Barry and Bobby were introduced to a local celebrity, a very beautiful mid-twentyish full-blooded Indian woman who was the meteorologist for a local television station. She had a gathering around her all night.

In order to get a pool table, it was required that you put a quarter under the rail in sequence with other people in line to play. The winners would stay on the table while the challengers would pay for the game. The losers had to buy a round of beer for the winners. Two teams were established: Barry/Mae and Bobby/Ana. It didn't take long for Bobby and Ana to be off the table, but Barry and Mae held the table for the remainder of the night. The beers that the losers were required to buy for the winners were beginning to stack up on the adjoining table. Bobby and Ana were invited to help themselves.

With the four of them drinking the winning beer, the dark amber bottles of Budweiser continued to increase in number beside the adjoining table. It got to the point where Barry and Mae announced to the crowd to help themselves. As closing time was looming, the staff delivering the beer to the table suggested the champs accept poker chips that could be redeemed for beer at a later date. People were lined up around the corner to get a crack at the invincible duo.

They couldn't lose. Even the Weather Princess stepped up and had a free beer courtesy of Barry and Mae, the celebrities of the night. Ah, but all good things must come to an end. Last round was called and soon after, they were swept out the door along with everyone else. In the parking lot the happy crowd was saying their goodbyes as they got into their cars and headed home.

As much as Barry wanted to be with Erin, fate chose a different path. Barry and Mae were not only the winning team, but the best. Mae was still celebrating and didn't want to go home. She had another idea.

"Hey, let's go swimming," she said, as she ran for the staircase that was along the side of the casino, leading to the water below.

"Ah, but I didn't bring a bathing suit," said Bobby.

Mae just kept on running, followed by Ana.

Barry looked at Bobby, and said, "Cool, let's do this" and ran after them down the stairs. When they got to the bright moonlit pebbled beach below, they could see the silhouette of Ana and Mae peeling off their blouses, spilling their breasts, stepping out of their pants, and running into the water. A number of possible scenarios swam through their heads, no pun intended. Barry and Bobby stripped down and headed for the water in like fashion. The girls, being skilled swimmers, were swimming freestyle on their way out to a dock that was anchored about a hundred feet offshore. As they dove headlong into the water, the shock of its freezing cold temperature was numbing.

Breaking the surface of the water trying to get acclimated to the frigid water, an odd phenomenon was occurring all around them. The crystal-clear water was alive with microscopic, iridescent, glowing bits of multicolored particles that tailed and swirled in the vortices created by the motion of their bodies. It was almost too much to fathom considering their intoxicated state. It was surreal; it was an experience neither one had ever encountered coming from New England. They recalled being "engulfed in a flight of fantasia."

A trip without LSD! The girls were already on the dock, giggling and flailing their arms upward, yelling, "Over here, over here!" The girls later told them that they had just experienced bioluminescence that created an explosion of green-and-blue fireflies as soon as the guys jumped into the water. This phenomenon only happens when a number of conditions all come together at the same time. It has to do with plankton, water temperature, its angle, and the brightness of the moon.

Barry and Bobby swam to the wharf where the girls were waiting. The surface of the dock was covered with bird droppings, so rather than climb up on the wharf, Bobby was content to hold on to the side before contemplating the swim back to shore. Ana worked her way over to him. However, rather than hold on to the wharf, as he was doing, she opted to hold on to him with one arm around his shoulder. Like an octopus, she wrapped her legs tightly around his. If there was any doubt as to the girls' intentions, it was now coming into focus.

Meanwhile, Barry was engaged in an encounter of his own with Mae. As they were standing at the edge of the water, Mae grabbed his penis and in the excitement of the moment, she turned to him and said, "Not now, let's wait until we get to the house." The natural progression of things was in motion.

They returned to Brother's house. Upon entering they were met by Erin. Helen was there too, but she didn't come out from where she was to greet them. Barry and Erin looked at each other and both realized that any opportunity of them ever sharing a moment was lost. Mae had laid a claim on him and that was that. Mae suggested that the foursome go downstairs and watch some TV to no avail. Mae leaned forward saying that there wasn't anything on, and shut the TV off, leaving them in darkness, paired up, and sprawled out on the carpeted floor.

At the first sign of another day, Bobby was eager to move on. The situation with the girls wasn't anything that Bobby wanted to pursue. As much as he appreciated their warm welcome and everything that came with it, Bobby was getting antsy. He didn't want any long-term obligations—permanent, semipermanent, or otherwise. He felt Ana was longing for a relationship, one he was not willing to reciprocate. It was best that this be nipped in the bud.

On the other hand, Barry was willing to stay a day or two longer and never thought of his time with Mae evolving into a long-term relationship. It was the '70s and he was enjoying the girls' company and would have liked to have stayed a few more days to play pool and drink beer. But in Bobby's mind, it was time to go. They left that day.

Chapter 10

JOURNEYING BACK HOME

THE DEPARTURE FROM CANADA AND back to the States was a bittersweet moment. They would miss Canada's beautiful landscape, the serendipitous adventures, and the unique hostel experiences. The hospitality of the Canadian people ensured there would always be food to eat and a safe place to sleep. Yes, they would miss the people, the kind, generous, and loving Canadian people. But it was time to leave Duncan and make their way homeward, crossing the Salish Sea, the body of water separating Victoria and Port Angeles. True to his nature, Barry once again made up a sign to catch a ride to Victoria City, a thirty-one-mile distance, to catch the ferry to Port Angeles, Washington. The ride out of Duncan was easy and the driver was more than accommodating.

Luckily, they were dropped off right to the port of destination. The ninety-minute trip on the ferry to Port Angeles was an opportune time for them to figure out exactly what their plan would be once they arrived in the United States. The ferry would come ashore north of Olympic National Park, giving them enough time to weigh their options before deciding: Do they go east on 101, a populated region with more traffic flow? Or do they travel west, a scenic route along the Pacific Coast, but with fewer opportunities to catch rides?

Another thing to think about was their depleting funds. Money was getting low so they would need to get jobs to stay afloat even if it meant picking apples.

Barry and Bobby had heard about job prospects in Yakima, a small metropolis east of the Cascade Mountain range and southeast of Olympia. The area was rich with fruit, creating a need for fruit pickers. To give a better visual of the area, Bobby described it like this: "The Cascade Mountain range divides Washington State into distinct eastern and western regions, with exclusively distinct weather patterns different from each other. The area west of the Cascades has the highest precipitation rates in the country. This region averages only eighty-seven days of sunshine in a year's time. On the other hand, east of the Cascades, even though this region lies on a parallel that bisects the state of Maine, it is a virtual desert.

The reason for this is that the precipitation contained in the cloud cover emanating from the Pacific Ocean is unable to traverse the mountain range. As a result, the cloud cover and the precipitation stacks up against the western slopes, and is forced to spill its contents of rain, making the western side of the state gloomy and wet for most of the year. Conversely, precipitation is prevented from reaching the eastern side of the mountains in the Yakima Valley which lies in what is described as a 'rain shadow' because the rain rarely falls there. For some reason, tree-bearing fruit thrive in this climate."

Taking into consideration the availability of rides and the probability of earning money, they opted to make Yakima their target. The plan was to work for a week or two, earn some money, and continue south to California.

When they disembarked the ferry and were preparing to pass through customs the officer asked, "Do you have any plants, fruits, or vegetables?" Surprised by the question, a few moments were necessary to collect themselves. They did have a couple of bananas and oranges. Ever so conscious of where their next meal would come from and money being in short supply, they excused themselves, stepped out of line, and proceeded to stuff down these forbidden fruits. With a stomach full of bananas and oranges, they entered through Port Angeles and were back in the U.S. by early afternoon.

Port Angeles is a small town on the upper western peninsula of Washington State, west of the Puget Sound. The white-capped Olympic Mountains loomed to the south and Mount Rainier to the southeast. Their intention was to skirt the eastern edge of the Olympic Peninsula, head south toward Olympia, and then east toward Yakima.

Effortlessly slipping back into their travel routine, it wasn't long before a man driving a small red Toyota pickup truck stopped and gave them a ride. The guy appeared to be in his late twenties or early thirties. A few days of dark brown stubble covered his face. He wore old, faded jeans and a well-worn T-shirt, topped off with a weathered old ball cap. He stopped and asked them where they were going. They told him they were going to Yakima to find some work. He introduced himself as Jake and told them he was only going about fifty miles. Not a problem.

Barry slid into the passenger seat while Bobby, with both backpacks, climbed into the bed of the truck. It was a beautiful day. Huge Douglas firs stabbed the cerulean sky. After leaving Port Angeles, signs of civilization waned until there were none.

Listening to the blaring sounds of Santana, Jake proudly broke out his tin of marijuana, consisting of loose buds, rolling papers, and a few joints. He lowered the volume and looked at Barry with a huge grin. "This is my good homegrown stuff with no seeds, just buds." Holding the lighted joint, taking a long toke, and trying to stifle a cough, he offered Barry a hit.

Barry, used to growing his own pot at home, grabbed the joint between his thumb and index finger, took one long toke, and nodded.

Meanwhile, Bobby lay in the back of the truck, daydreaming, when the smell of weed wafted out the passenger window and under his nose. Barry called out to Bobby while cupping the joint in his hand as he held it out the window in his direction. Bobby took a hit and passed it back through the driver's window in a continuous motion until nothing but a roach remained.

PART II

A good friend is a connection to life—a tie to the past, a road to the future, the key to sanity in a totally insane world.

~Lois Wyse

Chapter 11

POULSBO

THE TRUCK STOPPED AT A fork in the road somewhere between Port Angeles and Olympia. Jake was going left onto Route 104 heading toward Puget Sound and the guys were continuing Route 101, the Olympic Coast Highway. They said their goodbyes and thanked Jake for the ride and (of course) for sharing his homegrown weed. Jake in turn wished them good luck in their travels and rode off. Unlike some of the hitchhiking experiences they had in the U.S.A., this first ride was definitely a good one with no hassles.

Scrutinizing their location, they noticed the terrain was different from anything they had encountered on their previous stops during their journey. They found themselves dead center in the middle of a forested wilderness, green and lush. There was nothing, no signs of human civilization except for the road signs at the intersection and the asphalt tarmac. The appearance of deer crossing the road close by was an uplifting sight. One white-tailed doe even stood and looked at them for a while before scurrying into the brush.

They felt encouraged when a couple of hundred feet away, they saw a stream. They would later learn it was a tributary of Snow Creek. The stream was located down an embankment from the road. It looked inviting—clean water to drink and wash in. It was late in the afternoon, and not knowing where the next ride would take them, they agreed this would be the place to set camp.

Near the creek, they found a spot in a high-grassed area hidden from the road. After clearing the tall grass that carpeted the meadow floor, they laid out their sleeping bags, preparing to settle in for the night. Bobby took out the Sterno stove along with a box of Kraft Mac & Cheese from the backpack.

Barry scanned the brook that was about three or four feet across. "This stream looks a lot like the brook I fished in for trout. Let me see if I can dig up some worms and catch a few."

Bobby said, "I'll start the stove while you catch us some fish to go with the mac and cheese."

While Bobby started cooking, Barry fished for trout with only a stick, hook, line, and little time to spare. Dropping his line into the water trying to lure a trout under the embankment of the stream, he was quick to realize he was not fishing in the Kancamagus mountains where he caught slews of native brookies the prior year. That year Barry spent weeks in a place he called the Chutes five miles up the mountain. It was a time before there were camping restrictions. It was a unique commune where youths gathered and spent a short carefree New England summer in an almost fantasy-like world, jumping into water chutes carved into granite thousands of years old by the river. This was not New England. He came up empty-handed; there would be no fish on a stick cooking over a campfire that night.

They were just getting comfortable as they ate their dinner when the temperature began to dip, prompting them to gather stones from the stream bed and collect any sticks and twigs available for a fire. They used the stones to form a circle to contain the fire and hot coals, then strategically placed the kindling to create an updraft, and finally lit the fire. Taking a step back and inspecting their work, Barry remembered the times he spent as a Boy Scout building campfires in the woods. For sure, this one was worthy of praise from any scout leader.

The fire was their first opportunity to be alone since leaving Massachusetts. While they lay talking round the campfire in the peace and solitude of their surroundings, the cool air was descending out of the hills and into the meadow valley below. As Bobby explained, "The conditions were such they would be blanketed in dew come morning. The cool air hovered above the ground in a thin veil of fog creating a thermocline, trapping the warmer air below it. This prevented the smoke from the fire going skyward. Instead, the smoke rose to the thermocline, maybe ten feet up, and traveled along the bottom of the thermocline at the mercy of the soft south breeze."

They absorbed the beauty of the evening, infused with the sounds of crickets and frogs. Then the tranquility of the moment was broken by the sound of distant motors, "a thumping noise only a single cylinder four-stroke dirt bike could make." Their peace was suddenly replaced with trepidation when they knew they were not alone. They could now see headlights coming closer across the meadow to where they were. The sound wasn't from dirt bikes but rather from two quads.

A man with a child was on one of the quads, and a woman with another child was on the other. Bobby's first thought was that they might be trespassing on somebody's land and that they were about to be given the "bum's rush." They stood to meet the family who came to investigate.

The man began with, "Boy! I sure am glad to see you guys; we smelled the smoke and thought that there was an out-of-control fire burning."

They told him they had hoped to stay the night and leave in the morning. After a brief introduction while feeling out the situation, he and his wife suggested that Barry and Bobby ride back with them to where they were staying.

They were assured that the accommodation would be better than what they had in the meadow. They really didn't have a choice since they were trespassers on their property. The proposition was too good to pass up. After dousing and snuffing out the fire, they piled onto the quads with the man, wife, and kids, and rode about a quarter of a mile through the meadow to where the family was staying.

They arrived at what appeared to be an old dairy farm. An old house was in the process of being renovated. The family was staying in a pull behind a camper trailer located near the farmhouse. Barry and Bobby were told they could sleep in the barn across the yard away from the house. The loft was full of baled hay, and they were welcome to bust open a bale to sleep on. Before leaving the barn, he looked at the guys with a grin and said, "Please, no smoking or open flames."

Sheepishly and with assurance, they told him not to worry. Thankful for the twist of events, they had a restful night's sleep in the comfort and security of the old barn.

The smell of bacon roused them from sleep. They wandered out of the barn to find an already awake family of four, busy preparing breakfast outside by their camper. Barry and Bobby were motioned over and invited to share their Sunday morning breakfast with them. Not having gone through all the introductions the night before, the man extended his hand and said his name was Rick Weatherill, and added he was the chief of police of a small town on the coast of the Puget Sound called Poulsbo. He definitely left an impression as he was remembered as a gentle man born with a humble and enduring smile. His wife, Harlene, was remembered as being just as endearing.

Soon after eating, Rick enthusiastically told Barry and Bobby about his plans to transform his old farmstead into an RV park. A couple of concrete pads with water and electricity had already been completed with excavations started on more. A stream that flowed down from the hills and fed into Snow Creek ran close to the side of the barn, where in years past, men would pan for gold. In the future he would encourage prospective campers to try their luck in the stream. Rick's kids couldn't wait to show Barry and Bobby the technique for how it was done. With still some gold left in the stream, they did manage to find a few tiny flakes. Bobby tried to save a few by wrapping them in tissue and putting it in his pocket. Barry, on the other hand, did a "catch and release" since they were fine flecks of dust. Now, if it was a nugget, that would have been different.

After Sunday dinner, while the family was packing up and getting ready to head back to Poulsbo for the work week ahead, Rick asked the guys if they would like to come to Poulsbo with him and his family. They lived in a rather large, two-story, turn-of-the-century wood-frame house, located up from the main street that ran north and south along the bay front. The house sat on a half-acre lot with an in-law cottage, separate from the main house in the bottom left corner of the property. Rick offered them a deal. If they were willing to paint the cottage, they could stay in it for free. Rick said that he would even point them in the direction of some paying work.

~~~

The cottage was tiny, approximately six hundred square feet. It was obvious that it had been unoccupied for some time and was used for storage. Upon entering the house, stacked boxes lined one side of the hallway making it difficult to move around. The bed in the single bedroom was surrounded with all sorts of flotsam and jetsam. Bobby had to tunnel his way into the room and clean off the bed to prepare a place to sleep that night. Barry felt more comfortable spreading out his sleeping bag in the enclosed four-by-eight-foot front porch. The guys briefly checked out the gallon cans of paint placed in the hallway along with brushes and stirring sticks before Rick left them to contemplate his offer to paint the outside of the house. At any rate, a free night's stay was a guarantee no matter what they decided.

As evening drew near, the mixture of boredom and curiosity prompted Barry and Bobby to walk down the hill to explore the Poulsbo waterfront. Poulsbo, a Norwegian town, meaning Paul's Place, was founded in 1886. They had their hearts set on finding a place where they could sit down behind a nice cold frosted mug of beer and mingle with the locals, preferably girls. They looked around and then at each other. Definitely no girls or open businesses, and the bars were closed for the night.

They took a deep breath and sat on a bench facing the harbor. In front of them was a marina with finger docks. Many of the boats docked there were liveaboards. Some of the windows were lit up with activity going on inside, but no one was out and about. The view was interesting, but any hope of having an evening conversing with young women was dashed. This sleepy seafaring town was more like a retirement community. Another long sigh. With nothing else to do, they walked back to the tiny house and settled in for the night.

Early the next morning Rick was at their door with an invitation to breakfast in the main house. He wanted to discuss a possible job opportunity. Rick gave Barry and Bobby the name and address of a business, along with the name of a contact person, where he knew they might find some work. "This is a geoduck processing facility," Rick told them.

"What's a geoduck?" asked Bobby.

"Yeah, what the heck is a geoduck?" Barry wanted to know.

Rick looked at them, and replied, "Hmm, a geoduck is a king clam, similar to most other clams. What makes them unique is they are found only on the West Coast and can live up to 168 years old. The majority of Washington's geoducks are found in Southern Puget Sound. They are considered delicacies in China, Japan, and Korea."

Excited to have such a captive audience, he went on, "The name geoduck is derived from an Indian dialect which translates to 'deep down.' They bury themselves in the mud, up to three feet deep, and send their necks up like snorkels."

He proudly added, "They are processed at a facility down on the commercial dock in town. Why don't you guys check it out? Tell the manager I sent you."

"I guess it's worth a trip just to see them for ourselves," said Barry.

"Yeah, and it might be a good option to earn money," Bobby agreed.

Rick looked at the guys and said, "Good luck, see you guys later this afternoon." He finished his coffee and kissed his wife goodbye before venturing off to the police station.

Barry and Bobby stayed behind with Harlene for a while and helped clean up after breakfast before setting out to find the geoduck plant. When they arrived at the dock, they were not prepared for what met their eyes. One never tires of hearing Bobby's rendition of what he saw.

Stacked one upon another, down the length of the

dock, were crates upon crates of creatures whose necks hung out and over the confines of the wire crates that contained them. These things looked like huge, deflated horse dongs. They looked to be two or three feet in length. The ones in the bottom crates were flopped out onto the concrete walkway as if they had made a slow-motion attempt to escape and had given up in exhaustion. The clams in the upper crates were reminiscent of a Salvador Dali painting. The one where the clocks are draped over differing objects, melting and dripping toward the ground. The clams' shells were totally inadequate to contain their bodies. The bodies hung out all around the circumference of the shells with the exception of the hinge area.

For Barry, walking through the building was unsettling and nauseating, especially since he rarely ate seafood.

Before even laying my eyes on these gruesome, prehistoric-looking clams with their necks hanging, the nasty smell made me want to gag. There was no way I could work in this facility and come out feeling or smelling good.

The job entailed cleaning the geoducks in preparation for consumption. The work environment in the processing plant was such that your feet would be wet all day, not good for their Frye boots. The provided rubber apron only partially protected the workers' clothing. Water flowed everywhere to rinse the area free of the by-product of the process. Sharp knives, clam guts, squirting water, and all sorts of slimy waste material collected on the wet cement floor. When they left the plant, their decision was firmly set without saying a word.

Walking back to Rick's house Barry and Bobby discussed what they wanted to do next. Working in the plant just wasn't going to happen and the idea of painting the house in order to sleep there was not going to make them any money, so continuing on seemed to be their best option. Plus, Poulsbo was no Cape Cod or Hampton Beach.

All things considered, they were truly grateful to Rick and Harlene for what they had given them and for the offer to stay in their cottage. Barry and Bobby don't always agree about when to stay or when to leave, but this time, there was no further discussion. Picking fruit in lieu of cleaning geoducks was obviously the better choice. It was time to move onward.

When they met up with Rick and Harlene that afternoon, Barry and Bobby told them they would be leaving early in the morning to head to Yakima to pick fruit. Rick and Harlene said they understood and were happy to have made their stay in Poulsbo comfortable. After dinner they walked the guys to the door and wished them safe travels. Barry and Bobby thanked them again for the food, a place to stay, and above all their friendship.

In retrospect fifty years later, both Barry and Bobby would be willing to try eating a geoduck.

Even fifty years later, Barry and Bobby continue to recall their unforgettable experiences with Rick, Harlene, and their children with gratitude and fondness.

In writing this book, they Googled his name to learn what had become of him. Rick's obituary mentioned how he had helped thirteen young people in his lifetime, but it really is fifteen including Barry and Bobby.

Chapter 12

HEADING TO YAKIMA
WITH FORTUNA

As PLANNED, THEY WOKE UP early. Fortified with the vision of more excitement that lay ahead they gathered their things, leaving Poulsbo behind. The next leg of their journey would be different, that is without fanfare. No naked swimmers. No smelly dogs. No drunken Irishmen or unsavory oysters. No naked swimming with girls in the bioluminescent ocean, or the likes of Jake toking his homegrown bud. With no pressing goal other than to secure a job in Yakima harvesting fruit, they settled into their routine, thumbs out. It wasn't long before a young man and his wife stopped and asked, "Where are you guys heading?"

Bobby replied, "We're heading to Yakima."

"My wife and I are taking a day trip to Mount Rainier. It's on the way if you guys want a ride," the man offered.

Without hesitation, they both got into the back seat. Much of the ride was taken up by Barry and Bobby reiterating their experiences on the road with a hint of what plans might lay ahead. They all became comfortable in each other's company, so they were not surprised when the couple asked if they would like to join them on the observation area up on the mountain. Lady Luck was still alive and well. As to be expected, they accepted. They traveled up the steep, winding, two-lane mountain road until reaching the visitor center parking lot. The visitor center was a large log cabin structure.

There was a large, corrugated pipe that led from the sidewalk to the entrance of the building. Barry turned to the young man and asked, "What's with the pipe?"

He went on to explain, "The visitor center is now below the snow line, but in the winter the snow covers this whole area. This pipe is in place so that people can gain access. A snowplow need only make a pass past the entrance of the pipe to expose the protected walkway to the building."

Still etched in their memory fifty years later, they recalled the sensations they felt that day. The air was cool and crisp and the sight of the snowcapped mountain peak looming high above was spectacular. They took pleasure in watching hikers embark from this area on their way toward the summit, people milling around their cars, gearing up for the trek. In the distance, a line of hikers could be seen, looking like a trail of multicolored ants, plodding along over the snow.

A few years later, when Bobby joined the army and was stationed in Washington, he and his wife would visit Mount Rainier. He described it this way:

The view from this elevation, combined with the clarity of the air, was beautiful to behold. Visibility stretched out hundreds and hundreds of miles. Other mountains of the Cascades were laid out before us to see. Ancient volcanoes, one of which, eight years, hence, would awaken from its sleep in May of '80, with rumblings and earthquakes to ultimately explode in a cataclysm that would blow a sizable portion of the mountain away, flatten whole forests of huge firs, and cover thousands of square miles with fine talc-like dust that blocked the sun and choked people's lungs—Mount St. Helens.

At the end of the day, having witnessed the unanticipated splendor atop Mount Rainer, they rode down the mountain with their amiable acquaintances. Since the couple was returning home to the Olympic Peninsula, the guys were dropped off at the junction of the summit road and the two-lane State Route 410 taking them to Yakima. The road was small, the traffic sparse. Dusk began to fall, and once again, the probability of getting a ride didn't look promising.

Walking on in the shadow of the tall forest, a house appeared in the distance. As they drew closer, it looked like the house was occupied. The interior of the house was lit, and a soft light spilled out of the windows illuminating the vicinity around the house. About 150 feet from the house was a barn. After a brief low-pitched exchange of words, they decided to scout out the barn to see if it were possible to gain entrance and quietly stretch out there for the night.

For Barry a good night's sleep in the barn took precedence over everything else. In his mind it would be a short overnight stay with no harm done. He wouldn't have to worry about wild animals or getting soaked with rain. Bobby, however, was a little more apprehensive and felt it was risky. He thought about the consequences of trespassing on someone else's property. The idea of a dog alerting the owners to strangers in the barn, who might in turn take the law into their own hands, crossed his mind. For Bobby, it was a real concern.

They decided to take a chance. With great stealth they opened the big barn door just wide enough for them to slip in. There was hay. The boards that formed the outside wall of the barn were not butted up together tightly. There was perhaps an inch or so of space between them, which allowed moonlight in, and gave them a broken picture of anything that might be moving along the outside of the barn. Before retiring, both agreed to be up and away very early, earlier than the people who lived there for sure. They set their mental alarm clocks. Even before the hush of night devolved into first blush, they got up and slipped away without a trace of their presence.

They walked down the same road taken the evening before. Due to it being so early in the morning in a sparsely populated rural area there was no traffic. They trudged forward on a band of asphalt that wound up, down, and around the forested mountain terrain that would eventually take them to Yakima.

Above the tops of the huge trees, the sky was beginning to lighten with the promise of a new day. Wispy pockets of morning ground fog hovered above the forest floor. Bobby describes it "like opaque ghosts slowly rising and twisting on the warming air gathering together and disappearing into the sky." The only sounds were bird calls foreign to what they had heard in New England amid the rustling of their bodies and the sounds of their footsteps as they plodded along.

They came upon a farmstead by the right side of the road. The land sloped away from the road steeply so that the barbed wire farmyard was well below the level of the road surface, giving them a glimpse of the tops of the outbuildings. The remaining property spread out across the wooded valley. The farmhouse was constructed with broad horizontal rough-cut boards. They saw a man feeding and tending his sheep and goats in the paddock closest to them. The farmer noticed the strangers and momentarily stopped what he was doing to study them, as they in turn studied him.

Barry was the first to speak. "Good morning!"

"Good morning to you!" He was a fit, weathered, middle-aged man. His skin was darkened and wrinkled from years of exposure to the elements. He wore a red-and-black checkered wool shirt and well-worn ball cap that could easily have been replaced months ago. Black rubber boots protected his feet from the mud in the paddock. Still holding a pail of feed in his hand, he cordially asked questions as to where they were going and how they happened to be where they were.

They answered his questions courteously, never making any reference to sleeping in his neighbor's barn. They were surprised to learn that there was a mountain lion lurking about. Apparently, the predator had killed some of his livestock over the past week. Given the opportunity, he was looking forward to dealing with it, to put a stop to the carnage. Looking at Barry and Bobby, the farmer reiterated the danger the mountain lion posed and advised them to be careful on their seventy-mile trek to Yakima. They thanked him, bid him adieu, and continued onward.

They were prepared for the worst, three days of walking to Yakima, but hoped for the best. And once again Dame Fortune showed her gracious face. In the quiet of the morning, off in the distance, they could hear the sound of an approaching vehicle. In response to Barry's extended thumb and Bobby's smiling face, the car slowed to a stop. With a snap in their step, they walked up to the car, greeted the man behind the wheel, loaded up, and were on their way to Yakima.

The road to Yakima was a myriad of changing elevations and winding curves with scenic overlooks and beautiful vistas. The first half of the route was predominantly up in elevation. They were passing through the Snoqualmie Pass region. Cresting the pass, the road began the winding, steep decline down into the Yakima Valley. There was a noticeable change in the flora, in that the green of the western side of the mountains gave way to the brown and more arid types of vegetation of the east. They were dropped off on Main Street, Yakima, a moderate-size city with a population of around forty-five thousand people. The sudden change of scenery was stark compared to the days spent in the verdant rain forest where they had spent most of their time in western Washington.

The guys began to walk down the street of the city trying to get their bearings and figure out who they could ask to find work picking fruit. It was early afternoon and Barry thought it was a good opportunity to meet the locals, find short-term work, and be directed to a place to stay the night. Before they could find anybody to ask, a group of four evangelists approached them. They were greeted by a woman with stunning blue eyes, the shape and color that draws attention. As she was handing a leaflet to Barry and Bobby, she introduced herself as Ella.

In the next breath she asked with genuine concern about their salvation, "Are you saved?"

They all stood there intently waiting for an answer.

"I've been baptized, so I guess I am," Barry replied.

Bobby went on to say, "We aren't particularly religious, but we would be willing to listen to what you have to say." The guys conveyed how they had just arrived in town. They were looking for some short-term work picking fruit and later would work on finding a place to stay. Ella invited them to stay at their commune.

Since the evangelicals were looking to add members to their flock and since Barry and Bobby needed a safe haven for the night, it was a win-win situation, and they readily accepted her invitation. The newly formed group walked along the city streets to the edge of town, no more than a mile. They arrived at the two-story 1940ish house. The lawn was green and well-manicured on both sides of the walkway that led to the front door. Porch swings hung from the ceiling on either side of the door. The place was well maintained. Once inside, they found themselves standing in a large parlor.

Through a doorway, straight ahead and to the left, was the

dining room where three picnic tables were arranged. To the right was the kitchen area, where food was prepared. Ella led them into the kitchen. In the center a man turned and asked, "Who do we have here?"

Ella responded pointing a finger at each individual, "This is Barry and this is Bobby."

"I am Phillip. Welcome."

Phillip listened intently as Ella quickly explained their situation. They were invited to stay as long as they adhered to specified conditions. In return for a place to sleep and food to eat, they would be expected to perform jobs around the property. To the right side of the house was an extensive garden that the community relied upon to supplement their foodstuffs. Both were tasked with weeding the garden, a job Barry thoroughly enjoyed.

When supper was called, the members gathered in the dining room and sat at the picnic tables. Barry and Bobby were then introduced with a short explanation of having been found by Ella while serving her evangelistic duties in town. Following Phillip's lead, everyone lowered their heads and gave thanks to God for all of the blessings that had been bestowed upon his humble assembly. With thanks, they all said "Amen" and began to partake in the meal. The whole-time during dinner, Phillip kept a wary eye on them.

Homemade bread with herbal butter was on the table, and then the dishes of food were brought and passed around. The food, consisting of a smorgasbord of different garden vegetables painstakingly prepared, was awash with flavor. To Bobby the meal was a godsend and to Barry eating fresh produce reminded him of his own garden back home.

Thinking about the days ahead, this nutritious feast was just what they needed. Cleanup duty after dinner fell to others since the guys had weeded earlier in the day, thus leaving them free to wander about for the evening.

Across the street and down the road to the right of the commune was a drive-in movie theater. Ella and two others from the group suggested that they all go to the drive-in to see the movie, Jeremiah Johnson. The drive-in management didn't mind if a few people from the commune sat on the outskirts of the theater as long as they stayed out of sight. Ella's companions, a couple, suggested that they get some beer from their trunk first before heading to the drive-in.

Their car was easy to get to, given that it was parked beside the commune property. Of course, drinking beer on the premises was certainly not allowed; however, since they were no longer on holy ground, they found it too alluring to say no.

"Yeah, some beer sounds fine!"

They sat on the ground and watched the show. Barry, who was seated next to Ella, was attracted to her but had no intention of getting involved with anyone—let alone Ella from the commune. He had no intention of being saved that night or any night.

After the show, they dodged the cars that were scrambling for the exits and returned to the commune for the night. Before the last light was extinguished in a whispered exchange of words, they agreed unequivocally that life in a commune was not for them. Sleep was elusive that night. Even before the first rays of light poured into day, Barry and Bobby surreptitiously walked away from the commune feeling gratitude for being well fed and well cared for if only for a short patch of time.

Having discovered that the fruit wouldn't be ripe for another month gave them the perfect excuse to exit. So, they left Yakima behind and set their sights on traveling south to California.

Chapter 13

THE NEXT LEG OF THE JOURNEY

THERE WAS NO SLOWING DOWN. With one foot in front of the other, and with Bobby's thumb extended and Barry's sign for Sacramento in clear view, they steeled themselves for the next chapter of their journey. The future looked good. They had a little less than half of their money and needed no more than five dollars a day to live. A young man driving a "'65 Electra 225 convertible" pulled over. The day was sunny and the blue sky was scattered with thin feathery clouds like angel wings. It was a perfect day to ride with the top down. As soon as Bobby laid eyes on the car it reminded him of the car his principal, Mr. Henderson, had in grammar school. Even the burgundy color was the same.

The man decelerated and looked at the black chunky word **SACRAMENTO** written on Barry's sign. Rolling down the window after eyeing each guy, he blurted, "I am heading there myself to visit my mother who lives in Sacramento. Why don't you guys get in!"

Bobby always appreciated old Buicks. The big "430 cubic-inch Buick with its Wildcat V8" pulled away from the curb, "torquing" its way up to speed and headed for California. Bobby was seated in the front passenger seat and Barry sat in the rear.

Somewhere along the way, Gary, the young man, pulled out a

big ol' jug of cheap red wine that was generously passed around. By this time the music was blaring. The Guess Who's "American Woman," Rod Stewart's "Maggie May," and Led Zeppelin's "Stairway to Heaven." He finally turned the music down and told them he was on leave. They learned he was stationed at the Yakima Firing Center, a training area for all sorts of army-related live fire exercises involving tanks, artillery, and even rotary wing gunships. Two years later, Bobby would be traveling this same road and would also serve at the Yakima Firing Center after he signed up for the army.

Riding along, the conversation began to wane, so he turned up the volume. Bobby checked on Barry in the back seat, who had been quiet for some time due to his bout with car sickness. He was sprawled out across the seat, face up to the blazing sun, his fair Norwegian skin akin to the cherry-red wine they had just finished.

The trance-inducing lull of the ride was broken when Gary decelerated and asked, "How would you guys like to visit the old volcano, Mount Hood? It is a minor detour from the route we are taking." His invitation piqued their interest, and they accepted his offer.

As with Mount Rainier, there was a service road that wound its way up to an observation parking area, where they stopped and got out of the car to take in the view. It was a popular spot, as there were many cars, with people taking in the sights. The whole area was strewn with black volcanic rock. There were also families of small rodents, resembling chipmunks, scurrying all over the place munching on uneaten handouts people had thrown to them.

Gary was pressed for time so the trip up to Mount Hood was brief but well worth everyone's time. The ride back on Route 97, a rural two-lane state road, was pleasant enough. However, the Buick periodically overheated, necessitating occasional stops to add water and allow the engine to cool down.

Bobby noticed a field of high grass, then asked, "What's growing in the field?

Gary said, "That's wheat. If you strip the heads of grain from the stalks and chew on it for a while, it will eventually turn into a gum. It tastes pretty good too. It has a nutty flavor. Do you want to try some?"

Not having eaten since early in the morning, they thought it was a great idea. Barry said, "Sure, I'll try some."

"Okay, let's give the ole gal a rest and a bit of water." He pulled the car over into a thin shallow easement between the road and the wheat. Grabbing a handful of wheat, Gary demonstrated how to strip the heads of grain from the stalks, then how to separate the grain from the chaff. He placed the heads of wheat in the palm of his hand, covered that hand with the other, and rubbed the heads back and forth between his palms, effectively separating the wheat from the chaff.

After doing that for a bit, he held out his hand and began to gently blow on the separated wheat and chaff. The chaff would blow away, leaving a handful of grain. Barry and Bobby followed suit and popped the grain into their mouths and chewed on it for a while. Looking at them chomping on a great big mouthful of wheat gum, Gary smiled, and said, "When I was a kid, I would gather a handful of grain and chew it until it morphed into puttylike gum. Man, I could chew it for hours." The guys were surprised at how much they actually enjoyed it and how chewing it satisfied their pressing need for food.

The melting sun gave rise to the crescent moon and a smattering of stars signaling the changing of the guard. Barry, who'd been sleeping in the back seat for most of the day, was entrusted to take control of the wheel until the wee hours of the morning. They were now nearing Sacramento. Gary, familiar with the area, took the wheel in order to navigate the twists and turns that led to his mom's house. A few streets short of arriving there, he stopped the car and explained that he was sorry, but he couldn't take them to his mom's place. Knowing his mom, he knew she might flip out if he brought two strange hitchhikers into her house.

Gary was not without a plan. He offered to drop them off a few streets away and told them to leave their packs in his trunk while he visited Mom. He reassured them he would be back for them soon. He drove off. Like idiots they had just realized Gary had left with their backpacks. As he turned the corner, Barry and Bobby began to reassess what they had just done.

Bobby turned to Barry, and said, "Shit, what if Army Guy doesn't come back?"

Barry responded, "We're fucked!"

"If he doesn't come back in a reasonable amount of time, we'll go looking for it. If he is in this neighborhood, that Buick won't be too hard to find."

From where they stood, they saw what looked like a small grove of oranges and decided to check it out. Barry and Bobby had never seen orange trees before since oranges never grew in Massachusetts, but they were right! It was an orange grove. Their confusion at first was because the setting hadn't seemed right. Who would expect to see a grove of oranges on the outskirts of an urban area? The grove was surrounded by an eight-foot fence.

Intrigued, the guys watched the fruit pickers through the fence harvesting the oranges while one eye watched for Gary to make his promised return. They watched intently as an armed machine gripped the trunk. A hopper was deployed around the circumference of the trunk and then the arm began to shake the tree vigorously causing the fruit to fall into the hopper. Pretty cool.

To their relief, Gary did come back. From a prior conversation Gary knew the guys were looking forward to catching a glimpse of the huge sequoia trees and maybe swing through Angels Camp to look up their best friend, TC's, brother named Bob. Within about fifteen minutes Barry and Bobby were dropped off at the intersections of Routes 16 and 50.

Riding through the harsh sunlight and driving through the night left Barry drained. In addition to experiencing dehydration, his eyes felt gritty as if a handful of fine sand had been flung into them, making it painful to open them. Bobby, seeing his ailing friend, took on the task of thumbing for the next ride. The wait was unexpectedly brief; they were picked up from the outskirts of Sacramento and driven all the way to Angels Camp, a ride of about eighty miles.

They found themselves on the edge of Angels Camp, a touristy town with historic picturesque buildings lined up on one side of the street. Across the strip of buildings and down an embankment of about ten feet, they spotted a crystal-clear creek, Cherokee Creek, that paralleled the street above. Carefully climbing down the steep embankment, abutting a small bridge spanning the creek, Barry found relief. The cold refreshing water was a welcome friend. While Barry was imbibing in the generous offering of the creek, Bobby came to the sudden realization that their behavior would be contrary to the accepted norms of this town. Bobby was looking up at the people on the sidewalk who were looking down at them, literally and figuratively.

Upon entering Angels Camp in Calaveras County neither Barry nor Bobby had any idea they were entering a town rich with history. Angels Camp was filled with unexpected surprises. The first surprise was Angels Camp was not a camp, but a town. In fact, they learned that Angels Camp was named after a New Englander named Henry Angel. Apparently, he started a trading post in the camp during the Gold Rush of 1848. The brick and wood buildings were constructed close together on one side of the street and were reminiscent of the old 1800s.

By the '70s they were neatly refurbished and colorful, yet still maintaining their uniqueness as an old mining camp. There was the Mercantile established in 1860, the Utica Hotel (1881), a bakery, gift shops, and restaurants. More importantly, it was the birth of Mark Twain's literary career. Hearing tales of the 49ers using their idle days catching frogs and betting which frog could jump the farthest, Mark Twain recreated his first short story, "The Celebrated Jumping Frog of Calaveras County," published in 1867. In 1893 Angels Camp started the first Jumping Frog Contests and in 1928 the first modern contest began and continues to be held every third weekend in May. Seizing on Mark Twain's popularity, the town changed from a mining town to a tourist attraction. Having missed the date, the guys had to settle for looking at caricatures of frogs displayed throughout the town.

T.C.'s brother, Bob, was stationed at the Calaveras Ecology Center, not far from Angels Camp. He was a smoke jumper. The Ecology Center was a few miles from town. When they got there, they were told Bob C. was on leave and wouldn't be back for a while. Time to move on.

There are always trade-offs in this game called life. They might have missed a chance meeting with T.C.'s brother, but they gained a whole new perspective of Angels Camp. In hindsight, their decision to change course to meet Bob impressed upon them the power of fate leading to the events for the rest of their journey. Once again, they walked north to the outskirts of town. Barry took on the job of extending his thumb. A "Ford Bronco" pulled over. Inside the Bronco were three young girls with a young man at the wheel. Looking at his long blond hair and mirrored sunglasses, it was difficult to determine if he was a surfer or a hippie, but one thing for sure—he was not very social. The girls, on the other hand, were very eager to meet these two long-distance travelers.

The door swung open. Nimble and quick they managed to squeeze into the back seat with two of the girls. Of course, one of them sat on Bobby's lap much to his delight. Upon closer inspection, he noticed she had short shiny dark hair, blue eyes, pale skin with "pronounced ruby lips." Bobby described her as "a small but compact little beauty with an engaging personality." As he freely conversed with her, Barry engaged himself with the other girls all the while Driver Man remained aloof keeping to himself.

The girl in the front passenger seat informed them that they were going to stay the night at a chalet owned by her family and asked if they would like to join the party. Without even using one's inference skills the answer was a given.

"Sure!" came their retort as visions of three guys, three girls, a case of beer, in a posh ski chalet, nestled in Sierra Nevada, danced in their heads. This could be a rather enjoyable evening.

Arriving in Bear Valley, a large marquee of a bear about ten feet tall, carved out of a tree trunk, greeted them. The Bronco turned left off the main road and then onto a smaller paved road that led upward in elevation through a forest of huge fir trees. After maybe a quarter of a mile the Bronco turned left off the paved road onto a gravel driveway. About three hundred feet the chalet, an impressive A-frame structure, came into view. The kitchen, dining room, living area, and bathroom were on the ground floor. Upstairs were loft bedrooms and another bathroom.

Outside, the view from the porch was spectacular. The front of the building overlooked the valley to the east, which stretched for miles and miles of forested wilderness.

The evening was filled with lively conversation. The stereo was tuned in to a late-night rock 'n' roll radio station, creating a perfect atmosphere to the evening. Many beers were consumed. The evening was flowing along very nicely except for Driver Man, who continued to keep to himself. The guys attempted to converse with him, but their efforts fell flat.

Bobby continued to gravitate toward Red-lipped Lap Girl, and they were getting on rather well. As the evening wore on, Driver Man said he was going to bed and headed up the stairs, motioning for Red-lipped Lap Girl and Front Seat Girl to accompany him. This left Barry, Bobby, and the remaining girl downstairs. It appeared Driver Man was enjoying himself with two girls up in the loft. This turn of events definitely put a damper on their expectations.

The Other Girl who was left downstairs became a bit stand-offish, perhaps to signal she was not interested in a ménage à trois, and she made her point unabashedly clear. They certainly understood her feelings and acted in a way that posed no threat. With the hour getting late, it was time to get some sleep. Other Girl rolled out on the couch; Barry and Bobby settled for the floor.

Not long after they had settled in, Front Seat Girl, whose family owned the house, came to the railing of the loft bedroom above announcing something about her parents and they would have to go. So, at about two in the morning, bewildered and without malice, they gathered their things and left the house. They walked up the gravel drive to the hard surface road and decided they would have to finish out the night there on the side of the road. It was pitch-black and no signs of life anywhere. With heightened alertness, in bear and wildcat country, they moved off to the woods along the side of the road and sprawled out in the pine needles.

This was called Bear Valley for a reason. Needless to say, they didn't sleep very well. Every snap of a twig, every puff of wind rustling the trees overhead, every sound was fearfully scrutinized. They hunkered down with their sleeping bags over their heads as though they would offer them a barrier of security. Barry remembers putting his head deep inside the sleeping bag thinking, "If the bear doesn't see me and I don't see it, we'll make it through the night."

In the dampness of early morning, happy to not have been mauled and devoured by wild carnivorous animals, they rolled up their gear and walked down the mountain road to the main road about a quarter of a mile away to continue on their trek. Strange that they would be turned out in the middle of the night for no apparent reason after being invited to stay. No doubt, it had less to do with parents and more to do with aloof Driver Man.

Chapter 14

THE ROAD TO ZEPHYR COVE

CONSIDERING THE EARLY HOUR, MIDPOINT between Angels Camp, California and Stateline City, Nevada, on a small county road out in the middle of nowhere, Barry and Bobby were not surprised to find no traffic. So, they walked, and walked. A car or two might have passed them over the period of an hour or two until finally a car stopped.

"Where ya headed?" the driver asked. Toward Lake Tahoe was their answer. "I'm on my way to Zephyr Cove, north of Stateline City. You're welcome to ride along."

Eagerly, they accepted his offer. They shared their story of being asked to leave the chalet in the middle of the night. He said that he was curious as to why two guys would be walking along this deserted road so early in the morning. Now he had the answer.

As they drew closer to Stateline City, there were more and more signs of civilization until they were finally driving through the metropolis of Stateline City. It was a concrete menagerie of medium-height buildings, with flashy neon signs spelling out the names of the respective casinos that lined the main drag. This was a gambling town. People already crowded the sidewalks. Some were up to face a new day while others were winding down from a night of booze and gambling.

The driver told them that it was a favorite spot for Californians to come and gamble, as it was right on the border of California and Nevada. As mentioned before, Barry and Bobby were wary of large population centers knowing full well that bad things go on in these places. The uneasiness in their gut prompted them to ask if they could continue on with him to Zephyr Cove where he would be concluding his drive.

The need to know more about Zephyr Cove compelled them to ask more questions. He told them there was an RV park on one side of the road and a casino with a beach area behind it on the other side of the road. He went into detail about the long pier where a paddle wheel riverboat would take passengers for a tour of Lake Tahoe. He went on to say that sometimes the guys who manned the riverboat would take on hands to work on the boat or on the dock that serviced the boat.

The casino mainly patronized occupants of the RV park and the small hotel nearby, plus any travelers who wandered in. This sounded more to their liking. When he left them off, they were pleased to find it was just as he had described. On the west side of the county road there was a rather extensive RV park situated in a wooded area. Opposite the county road was the Zephyr Cove Casino. The architecture of the casino was that of a large log cabin. The building was two stories tall with the casino on the ground floor. The upstairs might have been for administrative purposes.

Barry and Bobby could see the lake from where they were dropped off at the front of the casino. The sight of the expansive aqua green water was an invitation for them to walk down the side of the building to the water's edge to take in the grandiose view of this beautiful lake. The beach was the perfect place to stretch out their limbs and relax for a while.

Most of the people at the beach were from the RV park across the road. There were lots of young kids and teenagers roaming about. Like most inquisitive teens seeing two young men who looked a bit out of the ordinary, they wanted to know more about them. After a brief introduction they told them that they were looking for a place to sleep for a day or two. A young man, perhaps sixteen or seventeen, who seemed to be the leader of a small group of mostly young girls suggested that they check out the RV park. There was a three-strand barbed wire fence that encircled the park that might lend itself to a cozy spot covered with pine needles on the back side of the park, just over the fence.

While they sat pensively taking in the sights, a young woman of about eighteen years old, who they later learned was named Becky, was walking toward them with her younger sister. As she passed, Bobby said hello as their eyes met. She said hello back as she kept a watchful eye on her sister. She told Barry and Bobby that she and her family were camping for the week in the RV park. The guys told her that it was suggested to check out the accommodations just over the fence outside the confines of the park. They mentioned that they wanted to go into the casino to have a look around but were in a bit of a dilemma since backpacks were not allowed in the casino. Surprisingly, she readily volunteered to ask her parents if they could leave them at their campsite. They followed her back to meet her parents. The girl's mother agreed without hesitation to let them leave their stuff.

With backpacks safely stashed away, Barry and Bobby took the opportunity to roam about the casino, a novel experience for both. As evening was drawing closer the crowd began to fill the casino. The place was dimly lit. The main light source was from the backing lights of the one-armed bandits—slot machines—of which there were many. Four long rows of slot machines were positioned back-to-back.

People hoarded machines, playing four or five at a time. They would sit on a stool stretching a leg, placing a foot on another stool to take position of all the machines to ensure they would hit the jackpot. If anybody attempted to play a hoarded machine, a verbal warning from the hoarder would ensue. "Hey!! I'm playing that machine!" Another oddity was that many people playing the slots had their hands and half of their forearms blackened from handling silver coins, nickels, dimes, quarters, and half-dollars that were in circulation in those days. These were the hard-core slot machine addicts who would sit in front of the machines, day and night, dreaming of hitting the big one.

Like a vampire den, with night enveloping, the casino resurrected. The place was packed. The air was alive with the pinging and ringing of slot machines, the clacking and clattering of roulette tables, and the loud murmuring of an excited crowd. As long as a person was actively gambling, highballs (whiskey and water) were freely given by roving waitresses balancing trays topped with glasses filled with the golden liquid. No doubt, it was a tactic by the casino knowing that drinking alcohol would definitely bolster the gambling boon by lowering a person's inhibitions and encouraging them to continue throwing their money away in a futile attempt at coming out ahead. Casinos are not in the business of giving away money.

Barry and Bobby settled in to play the nickel slots. For one nickel, you could play one line. Three digits left to right in the center. For two nickels you could play two lines. For three you could play all three lines. For four and five nickels all three lines could be played, plus two diagonals. They were soon feeling the buzz of the free highballs. Amazingly, they were actually ahead from when they first started to play, but not by much, maybe up a dollar or less. Along with this good fortune came a heightening of their spirits of excitement and plain ol' fun.

They soon began to rub elbows with women who were a bit older, perhaps by four or five years or so. To up their chances of winning, a plan was devised. On the first roll, the guys would put in the three nickels while the ladies put in two, and then they would do the opposite on the next roll. Whatever winnings might come about would be split evenly. Hoping to end the night of gambling, drinking, and carousing in somebody's hotel room, they were sorely disappointed. After an enjoyable night at the casino, they decided to retrieve their sleeping bags from their camping friends and head over the fence to sleep it off.

In the morning, they enjoyed a hot shower in the campground bathhouse, brushed their teeth, and headed off to see what kind of mischief was awaiting. They brought their sleeping bags back to their camping family for safekeeping for the day and were greeted by Becky. Coffee and a light breakfast were offered, an invitation gladly accepted. After exchanging pleasantries, the guys decided to head back over to the beach for the morning.

They encountered the same group of teens they had met the day before. The young man showed the guys a flier that was being circulated in the casino that might be a cool undertaking for them to supplement their limited income. The flier advertised that if a husband and wife were willing to sit through a land sale pitch being held in a hotel conference room in Stateline City, that couple would be given fifteen dollars just for attending. Bobby needed the money, and fifteen dollars would give him a few more days to cover expenses. All he needed was a wife. Bobby immortalized his story.

When Becky and her sister came to the beach that morning, I told her about the flier. I said that I'd split the money with her. All she had to do was be my wife for the day. To my surprise, she accepted. That afternoon, the two of us hitchhiked to Stateline City. This was a first for her. She had never hitchhiked before. She trusted that I knew what I was doing and willingly went along for the adventure.

During the hours that we spent together, we got to know each other a little better. She was such a nice young lady. We arrived at the address on the flier and were seated in a large conference room along with perhaps a hundred other people. We watched a film about a proposed town in Florida that was in the development stage and that this was a great opportunity to get in on the ground floor. After the film and an upbeat speech from the MC, the crowd was set upon by a trained group of arm-twisters, eager to earn a commission by selling house lots in this proposed Florida town.

Our arm-twister was persistent. He showed us numerous maps of house lots and began his spiel. 'Oh, look at this one. There is to be a grocery store right next door! This is only going to go up in value! Such a good investment for a young couple such as yourselves!'

Becky was playing her part. 'Oh no, we're just newlywed and can't spend the money!' And then I added that I would need my father's OK on such a thing.

The arm-twister reached down beside himself and banged a telephone on the table and said, 'Why don't you call him?'

I made up some bullshit excuse as to why I couldn't call him and finally said, 'Hey, we came here for the fifteen-dollar voucher, and that's it!'

And with that, he reluctantly gave us a voucher for

the money and moved off to twist someone else's arm. As we were making our escape, Becky and I faced each other with mischievous smiles on our faces and walked out fifteen dollars richer for our efforts. When we were free of the building, we broke out into laughter holding on to each other stumbling down the sidewalk. We had fun.

With our mission complete, we hitchhiked back to Zephyr Cove. The voucher that was given to us was redeemable at a number of casinos in the area, of which Zephyr Cove was one. There was a catch though. The fifteen dollars was redeemable five dollars at a time every two hours and was to be paid in nickels. I assume that was so the money would go right back to the casino. After all, the casinos really don't expect you to win.

Becky refused to take her half of the score. She wanted me to have it saying that I needed it more than she did, and besides, she had an exciting day. I was hoping to play the slots with her that night with the money. Her parents wouldn't allow her to go into the casino though. Heck, there might have been an age requirement.

It is interesting to note that this was the first time Barry and Bobby had spent time apart to do their own thing. While Bobby was working hard with his make-believe wife to make them fifteen dollars richer, Barry, who had no desire to be subjected to a sales pitch, was perfectly content basking in the sun on the shores of Lake Tahoe. Intermittently, he would walk to the adjacent casino and play the nickel slots. This turned out to be a profitable venture since it gave him enough money for the day.

As evening approached, Barry and Bobby took up their station at the nickel slots, seeking out young women to team up with. Barry was holding his own against the machines that were geared to slowly separate you from your money. Bobby, not so much. Bobby's reserves were slowly dwindling.

Snaking through the crush of the crowd over the deafening noise of the machines, they ran into a familiar face, the cashier from behind the bar they had become familiar with over the past two days. She had finished her shift and was now free to roam about the casino on her own time. She played the slots with them and "sucked" down a few of the free house highballs. It wasn't long before she was feeling the effects of the booze and was now carrying on with reckless abandon.

The casino also had a cash bar where a variety of drinks could be bought. Bobby's cashier friend turned to him and said, "Bobby, if you are willing to run, I will buy a round of mixed drinks for the three of us." Cheap whiskey and water was getting old and the idea of a real mixed drink sounded good. "I'll have a Tom Collins and you guys get whatever you like," said the cashier as she handed Bobby a five. Then she added, "Oh, and Bob, on your way back, put the change in the Big Bertha machine."

So...as requested on the way back to find Barry and his cashier friend, Bobby set the drinks down and fed Big Bertha a dollar bill and pulled the long handle to set the wheels spinning. Big Bertha was a dollar slot machine that was as big as a two-story washing machine. The handle on the side of the machine was about four feet long. The wheels stopped one at a time, and as the third one stopped, a flashing red light and siren atop the machine began flashing and wailing, announcing to the whole casino that a sizable jackpot had just been won. Over the throngs of people busy gambling and talking, Bobby could hear his friend screaming uproariously even over the clamor of the crowd. She hastily made her way to him and threw her arms around him. The machine had hit one hundred dollars.

After the celebration, they returned to the nickel slots where

Barry continued to increase his winnings five cents at a time. Bobby was having a losing night. He played the slots until he was broke. Drunk and busted, Bobby announced to Barry and his cashier friend that he was done for the night and was going to jump the fence and roll out. Unlike Bobby, Barry was a frugal gambler. He set his goal each day to adhere to a five-dollar spending limit, guaranteeing he could buy food, cigarettes, and win another five dollars the next day. Not long after Bobby's departure, Barry found his way to his own sleeping bag content with his five-dollar earnings.

The next morning, Bobby was up before Barry. Confronted with the fact that he was now penniless was a major concern. He stumbled over the fence to the campground bathhouse to clean up and brush his teeth. While standing in front of the sink, looking at himself in the mirror, he put his hand in his pocket and discovered a nickel, one stupid nickel. After cleaning up, he wandered over to Becky's RV to secure his sleeping bag and backpack, which was leaning against Barry's.

Then he walked across the street to the casino for the free coffee, Danish, and muffins being offered. He thought, *What the hell, I'll put my last nickel in the slot, and that will be it, done.*

The first wheel stopped on a five bar. There's only one five bar per wheel, so the odds of getting a second five bar was statistically near impossible according to Bobby. But the wheel stopped, a five bar again. What a cruel tease! Now he was prepared for the disappointment that was sure to follow. Miraculously, however, the third wheel stopped, a five bar again!

Bobby was stunned, stupefied! In the moment of realization that he had won, he bellowed, "Oh my God! I hit it for five dollars!" The bell and flashing light alerted the floorwalker to bring him a voucher for his winnings. Looking at the five dollars in his hand he thought, *No more nickel slots for me. These five dollars have to see me all the way home, three thousand miles.*

Soon after Bobby's departure, Barry woke up thinking what a beautiful day in Lake Tahoe! After a quick shower, he headed to the casino where he saw Bobby sitting on the porch. He walked right past him and said, "I need some coffee, I'll be right back."

When Barry returned with his coffee, Bobby looked at Barry and in a serious tone said, "Barry, we gotta talk. I wanna leave. I'm done putting money in the slots. I'm done. I wanna go."

Barry, taken aback, responded with a quick retort. "Are you fuckin' kidding me? Bobby, one more night at least. We have a safe place to sleep, showers, washers, dryers, a nice beach with crystal clear water, and coffee every morning. I'm not ready to go yet. Do you really want to leave that bad?"

"I'm getting antsy. Just think about it. OK? But I need to get going."

Barry and Bobby wandered back to the campground to Becky's place to rearrange their backpacks, taking stuff out that was needed for the day. The family was now stirring about. Becky, her sister, along with their nasty Jack Russell Terrier mix dog just stepped outside and were heading to the picnic table. It was a small, wiry-haired mutt that was prone to yapping a lot. Mom was inside cooking breakfast.

They didn't want to linger so as to elicit an invitation to breakfast. Becky's mom had fed them the day before and they didn't want to appear as moochers. When Becky's mom invited them for breakfast, they declined saying they had just finished Danish and muffins at the casino.

"Well, you don't have to eat. You're welcome to sit with us if you'd like."

They accepted the offer, all the while Bobby stole glances at Becky, hoping to meet her eye.

The dog was still suspicious of Barry and Bobby even after three days of being with the family. When the dog thought no one was looking, he would cautiously sneak up and sniff one of the guys. If he found either one of them meeting his glances, he would bristle his razorback and hold his ground, softly growling out a warning, at which point Becky or one of the others would shoo him away.

But this particular morning was different; he took it up a notch. He sniffed his way to their backpacks, which were leaning against the trailer. Nonchalantly, he looked directly at Bobby, lifted his leg, and peed on his sleeping bag as if to say, "You leave my Becky alone."

Bobby said little, but his inner voice raged, *Nasty, ugly little shit. Ohhhh! You little son of a bitch!* Everybody thought it was funny in an embarrassing sort of way, everybody except Bobby.

Carrying their sleeping bags and backpacks, they walked to the laundromat. The washing machines were arranged under the overhang of the bathhouse. After Bobby's five-dollar windfall, he begrudgingly spent a dime for a box of laundry detergent, twenty-five cents for the washing machine, plus three more dimes for the dryer. Barry thought this was a good opportunity to do his laundry at the same time. They had not washed anything since the time they spent in Vancouver. When the wash was done, they transferred their loads into a dryer. Before doing so Bobby took a quick sniff to determine if the dog pee smell was gone and was glad to find the foul odor of dog urine gone and replaced with the familiar smell of Tide.

Thoroughly enjoying his stay at Zephyr Cove, Barry said, "Hey Bobby, while the clothes are drying, let's go to the beach."

"I don't want to leave our clothes or sleeping bags. Someone might come and steal them. We don't have enough clothes as it is."

"No one is going to take our clothes. You can stay and watch the clothes spinning around until they're dry if you want to. I am going to the beach."

Barry returned to the laundromat before the end of the drying cycle and mentioned that he had seen Becky at the beach cozying up to a blond-haired dude. Nothing more was said about Becky as they gathered their belongings and headed back to the RV park. Not taking any more chances, they placed their stuff on the yoke in front of the trailer hitch to ensure Becky's dog had no access to it.

They spent the rest of the day at the beach, going in and out of the cool pristine water, lying in the sun drying off, and watching the bikini-clad girls. The water was so clear fish were perfectly visible fifteen to twenty feet down. They dove off the paddle wheeler dock and were actually able to touch a fish or two. By midafternoon they were ready to venture off to the casino porch. Barry was so busy talking to the girls that he hadn't noticed Bobby's disappearance until he came back and said, "I'm leaving, I'm going to get my shit and I'm leaving."

"Bobby, it's not a good time. It's late in the afternoon. We won't have a place to sleep. Just wait until morning and I'll go."

But Bobby would not hear of it. He listened, but he was still determined to leave. He went over to the RV, got his stuff, and walked out to the road opposite the porch where Barry was sitting. In defiance, Bobby put out his thumb.

They stared at each other. It had now become a battle of wills. The first car went by, no ride.

Barry was still there looking at Bobby when the second car whizzed by. Barry was getting concerned. He did not anticipate Bobby being so unreasonable.

Barry crossed the street to where Bobby was standing. "What the fuck, Bobby? You can't wait until morning?"

"I told you, Barry. I'm leaving, I'm leaving. Either I'm leaving alone or you're leaving with me. What's it gonna be?"

Barry was no pushover, but he wasn't a fool either. Barry later recalled:

> *I was angry because Bobby's behavior was just a repeat of what had happened on the first trip in Illinois, and later in Vancouver. But I was in this for the long haul; we committed to this trip, and he was my best friend. I wasn't willing to let either one of us travel alone until we made it back home safely.*

This confrontation was the figurative fork in the road–either they would have to travel together or travel alone.

Bobby's emotional turmoil was festering, and it abruptly came to a head. The same thoughts swirled in his head: Becky, money, homesickness, and the idea of being so far away from home, the place where his girlfriend, Christine, was waiting for him. He wanted to head back home. Barry, on the other hand, was a free spirit with no commitments and his sole purpose of the trip was to roam untethered with no dictates of time or place. After all, it was his idea to explore Canada and make his way to California.

"Alright, alright, let me get my stuff."

They never did talk about it again. Barry went to retrieve his backpack and returned to the first car that stopped. A girl named Rhonda and her friend picked them up.

Chapter 15

THE HEART OF THE WOMEN

THE RIDE WAS SHORT. LOOKING at Barry in the rearview mirror, Rhonda asked, "Where are you guys heading?"

It was late in the day and since Bobby wanted to leave without delay, nothing was mapped out. All they knew was they were heading north. Reno was a possibility.

Barry replied, "We don't have a plan. Where are you heading?"

Rhonda told them that she was on her way home. The guys told her that they had just left Zephyr Cove and were looking for a place to crash for the night. There was silence as she studied them carefully in the rearview mirror and although conversation was limited, she reasoned these guys were safe.

Conversation resumed. She told them she lived with her mother about seven miles away in Glenbrook. Before taking a left on Old Highway 50 she stopped, turned around, and said, "You know, it's getting late. Why don't you guys crash at my house? We'll be there in a few minutes." They pulled into the driveway of a one-story house with cedar shake. They walked through a screened-in porch into the house. Rhonda introduced Barry and Bobby to her mom and told her they needed a place to stay. The vibes were not good.

They were asked to go back to the porch.

The guys could only imagine what was being discussed bringing home two hitchhikers whom she invited for the night. After much deliberation, the mom agreed to let them stay the night with the stipulation that these two unexpected guests sleep on the porch and be gone in the morning. After all, it was only three years after the heinous Charles Manson murders in '69. Therefore, it was understandable why she was not only suspicious but leery of her newfound visitors. They were more than happy to sack out on the porch. It certainly did beat sleeping on the hard ground in some unknown location.

By morning, Mom had softened and invited them to bacon, eggs, toast, and coffee. The conversation was light and congenial. They spent much of the morning sitting around the table talking about their adventures. Rhonda and her mom were captivated by their stories, and having never met anyone from New England, asked a lot of questions. It was time to go.

Before leaving to drop the guys off at the intersection of Old Highway 50, Rhonda asked Barry for his address so she could write to him. When the car stopped before the junction, they were alarmed to see a ghastly car wreck that had happened moments before. The police had not yet arrived. The scene was gruesome—a heap of twisted mangled metal, broken glass, and splattered blood. Just as they were getting ready to see what they could do to help, they heard the sirens and saw an approaching fire truck. Help was on the way, help far more superior than they could have offered. They left.

Hitchhiking on Highway 50, Barry and Bobby were picked up by a woman driving solo in a "'64 Chevelle station wagon." She told them she was on her way to Carson City.

She was an attractive blond-haired, blue-eyed woman in her

mid-twenties. She was wearing a backless beige halter top scooped with fabric below her throat, covering her collarbone. The halter top was tied by spaghetti strings at the base of her neck and above her waist. Before getting into the car, Barry mumbled to Bobby, "This ride should be interesting." And for Bobby it was more than interesting. Riding in the back seat Bobby could not resist the temptation to glance at "her beautiful breast" (typical Bobby) each time she lifted her right arm from her loose-fitting halter top.

The drive was relaxed and uncomplicated. Enjoying their company, she shared that she was going quite a distance, was concerned about her bald tires without a spare, and wasn't sure she would make it to her destination. When she mentioned that she didn't have a lot of money, Bobby suggested they stop at a phone booth and look through the Yellow Pages to find the closest junkyard to find some used tires. The woman knew the vicinity of a junkyard that Bobby told her about. It would be slightly out of the way, but she was more worried about a blowout than an inconvenience. Pulling into the yard, their first view was a pile of flattened cars stacked up on top of one another. One of the workers from the junkyard, said with a smile pointing, "Just over the fence is the Bunny Ranch, a whorehouse. Thought you guys might want to know."

Halter-woman looked at the guys with a coy smile, "You fellas wait here while I talk to someone who can sell me some tires."

Barry laughed, "Don't worry about us. We're not going anywhere."

Ten minutes later a yard worker came out with the tires. "Here you go, boys."

Halter-woman came out and said, "Can you put these tires on the car while I go back to the office and pay for them?"

It took the guys no longer than a half hour before the tires were on, rims and all. Done! But Halter-woman was still a no show.

Standing around Barry looked at Bobby, "What now? Halter-woman has been missing in action for the last thirty minutes."

Bobby without hesitation replied, "Let's climb to the top of the stacked cars and see this Bunny Ranch for ourselves."

For Barry, the experience of seeing a brothel was anticlimactic. While imagining the novelty of a legal sensuous experience involving all five senses, the reality of having no money set in. When they finally descended the pile of flattened metal scraps, they saw Halter-woman walking toward her car with a confident grin. "OK, boys, let's go."

To this day Barry feels they were manipulated by a woman who was well adept at her craft of seduction. They would have gladly succumbed to her if she hinted to engage in a ménage à trois. In the end, Halter Top-woman got what she wanted, the office manager got what he wanted, and the guys got a ride plus they got to see the brothel. Bobby, however, felt differently about his experience with Halter-woman. He felt he was simply helping a damsel in distress.

They pulled out of the junkyard and out onto State Road 50. "This is as far as I am going, boys," she said and dropped them off. This part of their story always left them wondering. Why the quick drop-off? They speculated since there were three brothels in the area, she may have been on her way to work.

Exiting the car, they found themselves at an arid, treeless intersection. On the right-hand side of the road loomed a golf course. Barry and Bobby cautiously walked into the lobby of the main building where they met the eye of the clerk who manned the desk. They politely asked if they could use the restroom. The clerk nodded and pointed a finger toward the bathroom where they washed up. On the way out, they got a drink of water from the bubbler, aka a water fountain, which was positioned beside a nickel slot one-arm bandit.

After standing on the side of the road for an hour or so, a quick decision had to be made. Barry could no longer tolerate the harsh burning rays of the sun and the searing dry heat. Again, this was the '70s and packing suntan lotion was never a consideration. The only protection from the midday sun was for Barry to shield himself behind a short shadow cast by the telephone pole on the side of the road.

"Bobby, I can't stay in the sun much longer. We have to do something here."

"Yeah, this is bad. Hey Barry, how about this. You hike south, I'll thumb north. Whoever stops first is the direction we will go."

"Sounds like a plan." Barry was beginning to rethink the idea of traveling south. Being from New England and never having experienced the dry heat of the desert he was in dire need of shade, lots of trees, not a solitary telephone pole. As fate would have it, a "'71 Volkswagen Super Beetle" was slowing to a stop. Bobby ran to the car, saying, "Hey, that's my buddy across the street. Can you wait a minute?" he asked the two young guys in the car. Bobby motioned to Barry. While Barry was gathering his backpack and making his way across the highway to the car, Bobby hastily explained to the driver and his friend that they were desperate to leave the area and were hitching in two different directions. He thanked them for stopping. Barry believes that ride probably saved his life in the Nevada desert.

Once on the road, the two young guys told them they were on their way to the drive-in theater in Reno which was about ninety miles away. At this point Barry and Bobby were willing to go as far as Timbuktu as long as they remained under a canopy of protection from their current source of misery.

The ride to Reno was relatively short, three hours. The drive-in movie theater was just off center city, an odd place for a drive-in. Another unusual feature they had not seen before was a spring-loaded apparatus that would lay down under the weight of a departing vehicle. Should a driver try to gain entrance through the exit lane without paying, the vehicle would have been met with spikes. Waiting in a line of cars to get into the drive-in, Barry and Bobby took the opportunity to express their gratitude for the ride, gathered their things, and closed the door behind them.

Arriving just before dusk in an unfamiliar city made it difficult to find a place to stay for the night. Unlike Canada there were no hostels, no safe havens of any kind, so they opted to continue east out of Reno. Instinctively, they both decided Reno or any city for that matter was not a safe place to be in. For Barry, the thought of being in a city surrounded by concrete structures with no greenery made him uncomfortable. For Bobby the image of city life with its hustlers, prostitutes, and homeless people trying to make a few bucks made him paranoid.

Shouldering their backpacks, Barry and Bobby began hitchhiking out of Reno when a cruiser pulled up. Two officers stepped out of the car, looked them over, asked a few questions, and concluded that they were not vandals, thugs or burglars. They were informed it was illegal to hike within the city limits. And the city limits happened to be twelve miles from which they stood. Once clear of the cops, they started walking. Knowing full well the consequences of thumbing within the city limits, they took the warning matter-of-factly and in turn cautiously stuck out their thumbs in the hope someone would stop.

First came the faint distant noise, followed by the appearance of an "old black '61 Ford station wagon." A middle-aged woman stopped with her six children ranging from about two to fourteen. She told Barry and Bobby she would give them a lift as long as they were willing to sit on the back of the tailgate. They gladly took her offer. They threw their backpacks into the back of the cluttered cargo area of the old station wagon and sat down on the tailgate with their feet dangling inches from the road's surface as the woman drove off.

The low guttural sound they had heard was due in part to its engine running on less than eight cylinders and its exhaust pipe near to falling off. The sight of Barry and Bobby was a novelty. The kids could not help staring at them inquisitively. In a short time, she pulled off the main road and into a convenience store gas station parking lot. With her kind demeanor she told them that this was as far as she was going and wished them well. They thanked her for the ride and waved to the kids as the old Ford chugged away.

Bugs were swirling around the fluorescent lights that outlined the soffits of the store. Not being customers, Barry and Bobby moved off to the side of the store to avoid attracting attention. There they would try to get their bearings and figure out what to do next.

Bobby, seeing an empty milk jug not far from a hose bib, started to fill his gallon jug with water along with Barry's canteen. Having experienced such arid conditions and the severe intensity of the drying sun, they didn't know what lay ahead. Meanwhile, Barry went over to grab two empty crates that were stacked on the side of the store and took out the map. They sat down on the overturned red plastic crates to contemplate their situation, studying the map. Where would they sleep? Would they hitchhike on through the night? Where were they exactly? Then as if their destiny was spun by the Fates, they began to hear the rumble of a locomotive engine off in the distance.

The sound of the diesels reignited their desire to hop trains; an endeavor they had discussed on numerous occasions was about to come to fruition.

Bobby looked at Barry and smiled. "What do you think? Let's go check this out."

With no plan in place Barry said, "Let's do it!

PHOTOS

Barry, July 1971 at the chutes off the Kancamagus Highway in the White Mountains

Bobby, December 1971

*The "Bluebird" van with and Mary and Karen out front...
our first cross country attempt*

Village of Seneca Falls, N. Y.
Police Department

P Nº   9266

GENERAL RECEIPT   6ⁿ72 - , 19 ____

Received of Robert P - Young $25.00

Twenty five dollars °°/100   Dollars

For Bail on Dealing with Fire Work

By Thomas H. Joy

Act 565

Title

*Receipt for Bobby's firework ticket in New York returning home from our
first trip attempt.*

Bobby's receipt from jail in Illinois

The start of heading home: The ferry from Vancouver Island to Washington State

June 1972, Bobby arrested on first trip in New York
for a case of M80s

October 1972, Celeste and Barry at Hampton Beach, NH

December 31, 1972, Bobby and Chris Wedding

*June 1988 Moving from Barre, MA to Deltona, FL
in Bobby's 18 wheeler*

August 1995 Barry and Bobby boating on the St. Johns River

August 1995, Barry and Bobby scuba diving trip in the Bahamas

May 2023 Tuesday with Barry

May 2023 Tuesday with Bobby

January 2024 Celeste and Barry's 50th Wedding Anniversary

PART III

True friendships withstand time, distance,
and silence.

~Isabel Allende

Chapter 16

THE THUNDER OF
THE MIGHTY DIESELS

TIME WAS OF THE ESSENCE, and without hesitation, they gathered up their stuff, crossed the road, and approached the train. At idle, the ground shook. They felt the pulse of the engines through the soles of their feet. They knew the train was preparing to leave, and soon. They scurried to find a spot to settle into. Up to this point in their lives, they had never hopped trains, so their first thought was to look for an open boxcar. Looking toward the front, they could see trailers sitting on flatbeds. Eventually somewhere, these trailers, also called piggybacks, would be picked up by a tractor and hauled off to a designated location.

Barry and Bobby walked from the front of the train all the way to the rear, checking every boxcar along the way, seeking an open door. Everything they knew about boxcars came from secondhand knowledge—television, books, pictures of hoboes—giving them the impression the boxcar was the only way to hop a train. Soon, they would find out differently. When double-checking the ground they had already covered on their way back to the front of the train, they found that every car was loaded and sealed with running reefer units. These cars contained perishable goods needing to be kept cold.

Hearing the revving engines, they ran to the front where the piggybacks were located. Surprised, they saw two people, a man and a woman, who were sitting up front under one of the trailers by the jack pins. From the lights of the railyard, they could see the woman was dressed in a thin cheaply made pair of pink polyester pants and a matching pullover blouse marked with holes, a few exposing her skin. They approached the couple; the woman greeted them in a hoarse voice. "Are you fellas looking to hop on?"

"Yes," was their reply.

"Well, you better hop on mighty quick. This train is preparing to roll."

Bobby was the first to join the duo. Barry was a little hesitant at first. Riding under a huge trailer weighing thousands of pounds with open sides on a flatbed exposed to the elements did not seem like a rational choice to make. But considering the calm demeanor of these two seasoned travelers, Barry thought, *What the hell, I've done more dangerous things in my life.* He jumped up on the side rail and hoisted himself on the flatbed. There he found his niche between Bobby and their newfound travelers.

Once well rooted in their places, the man took out a bottle of cheap port wine that lay underneath a threadbare, tattered light blue blanket. The man first offered a swig to his companion, then passed it to Barry and Bobby. They readily accepted. In kind, Barry took out his pack of cigarettes and handed one to each of his friends. Bobby offered them a light. In the glow emitted from his lighter, he could see the man's haggard appearance, probably due in part to drink and exposure to the harsh, unforgiving elements. His lady companion, in spite of her clothing, looked considerably younger. The soft lines around her eyes and deeper ones around her mouth gave way to her warm smile. Comfortably sitting and waiting patiently for the train to leave, stories were told. Between swigs and smoky exhales the couple, Percy and Grace, related their experience staying at the Salvation Army Mission in Reno.

"Damn scoundrel at the mission stole our suitcase with all of our stuff!"

Grace interjected vociferously, "Yeah, and he nabbed our precious puppy, Pickles! Son of a bitch!"

Barry and Bobby had to wonder. What type of person would steal Percy and Grace's puppy?

So now, they were in hot pursuit. "I heard through the mission grapevine who the perpetrator is, and Gracie and me is planning to go to Ogden to get her."

"Yeah," Grace agreed. "She ain't just a puppy, she's kin."

Road maps were given away freely at gas stations in those days and proved to be most valuable, some maps better than others. For instance, Gulf road maps not only had highways, but they also had railroad tracks mapped out. Armed with a simple compass and a Gulf road map there was no reason to wonder as to your whereabouts. They knew from their travel mates that the train was going to Ogden, Utah, a city just north of Salt Lake City. According to the map, the distance by highway from Sparks on Route 80 to Ogden was 548 miles.

After some time had passed, the brakes were finally released. Bobby, the locomotive enthusiast, recalled every moment of that day, hopping a train in the summer of '72.

The sound of pressurized air raced from the compressors with a hisssss through all of the cars to the rear of the train. The train jolted backward a few feet sending a violent wave through every car in succession to the rear of the train, only to immediately stop, followed by an equally violent jolt forward. Four mammoth diesels, in perfect unison slowly spooled their incredible inertial mass with

*a rhythmic lub, lub, lub, lub sound, increasing in cadence
until maximum rpm was achieved. The generators, with
a ghoulish whine, were rising to the task of feeding the
electric drive motors. The train, with a groan of protest,
crunched and squealed and struggled to gain speed.*

*And gain speed it did. The cars began a slow side to
side dance as they swayed back and forth on coil spring
suspension. The clack of hardened steel wheels rang as
they rolled over the expansion joints between the rails. The
deafening sound of screaming diesels so near to our front,
combined with other sources of noise associated with the
onward charge of the train, made any further conversation impossible.*

As the train attained cruising speed, the lack of any type of
wind protection was becoming a problem. In dry desert climates,
daytime could be extremely radiant and hot; however, nighttime
was quite the opposite. Their hosts were now hunkered down behind the thin blue blanket and were gathered close together in a
vain attempt to stay warm. Barry and Bobby had taken up residence
on the leeward side of the trailer wheels that blocked the wind.
Wrapped in their sleeping bags, they might have been warmer than
their companions, but very cold nevertheless in the face of frigid
gale force winds.

Everyone lay in solitude on the hard steel floor with their own
thoughts. Barry, with his head buried deep in his sleeping bag, was
quickly lulled to sleep by the rhythmic sound of the train riding over
the track expansion joints–*clickety clack, clickety clack, clickety
clack.* Bobby, on the other hand, was too excited to sleep. He recalls:

*In situations like this, sleep is attempted, but you
don't really sleep. There is too much concern for safety
among the unknown dangers that might steal you away*

in a flash. After wandering off into a pseudo dream state,
reality rushes back to the here and now with a start. There
were occasional blasts of the train's horn along with the
clanging of crossroad alarms with flashing red lights that
would suddenly appear and just as quickly be gone.

After passing through a short tunnel and settling into a steady rhythm, Bobby finally succumbed to sleep. Slumbering through two hundred miles, they were all roused from sleep when the sun made its appearance, bringing with it a wave of hot, moist less air. The incessant noise from the engines hindered any meaningful conversation. Intermittently, Percy and Grace would speak inaudibly, but for the most part everyone just looked at the scenery as it whizzed by. Since being on the road never knowing when or where the next ride would take them, the guys enjoyed their unexpected respite, grateful to have the opportunity to sit and mindfully explore their surroundings, so vastly different from other places they had been.

When a train finally stopped on the sidetrack, it was close to noon. The foursome sat under the piggyback surveying what could aptly be called a semiarid desert.

Barry turned to Bobby, and said, "Man, I gotta take a piss."

"I am right behind ya! This place looks interesting."

Telephone poles ran parallel to the tracks casting shadows about one foot in length. Standing in the shadow of every single pole was a jackrabbit with its long ears and long legs, scrutinizing their every move. To the left of the train, across the main track was a long-forgotten corral. One could speculate it was probably used to load cattle onto the trains many years ago. Adjacent to the corral was a rusted water tank with a worn-out windmill, many of its vanes missing, others bent.

Outside the train, the blazing sun was not welcoming. No one was sure how long the train would idle so Barry and Bobby were overly cautious about time, making sure they could run back to the train. Both knew running through the sand in their heavy Frye boots would be a challenge to say the least. Walking just about a hundred feet away from the train, they noticed mummified skeletal remains of jackrabbits scattered about. On closer inspection, the many carcasses lying in the extreme heat were covered with skin and fur. There was no telling how long those bodies had been there. Barry wondered if they had been poisoned or shot for sport; there were just too many to be a coincidence.

After a good twenty-minute stretch and a chance to explore their strange surroundings, they didn't want to press their luck, so they headed back to the train. Within a short time after settling into the shade of the piggyback, they were not prepared to see what came next. A train about a mile long traveling on the main line, going in the opposite direction flew by at top speed. The blast of a klaxon horn increased in pitch and volume as it approached—*ding ding, clack, clack, woosh*—until the deafening noise faded as it moved rapidly away.

If that train had come upon them as they were walking around investigating their surroundings, they could have been cut off from their piggyback. Their train would have left them standing, separated, abandoned in the high desert, where they might have met the same fate as the animals whose dried bones littered the area. Minutes after the other train had passed by, the mighty diesels stirred from their idling rest, jerking the train back to life. Clanks, squeals, and groans filled their ears as the train began the forward charge once again.

On the north side of the tracks and down the steep embankment lay evidence of a derailment that happened days before. Multiple cars lay on their sides, roofs broken open, and contents strewn everywhere, reminding the guys that hopping trains could have dire consequences. Work crews with heavy equipment were still actively cleaning up the mess. They noticed that the roadbed on which they were traveling was new with fresh crushed granite and new ties. It was now obvious the derailment was the cause of the new construction. The brief stop miles prior was intended to let the train, going in the opposite direction, pass.

Not far ahead lay the Great Salt Lake. The view was awesome. They were captivated by the colors they could see on both sides of the track: to the north the water was reddish pink, to the south the water was aqua blue/green.

As they stared at the water they were puzzled as to the reason and later discovered it was because the water north and south of the track differed in saline concentrations. The first track was built on a trestle and in '59 a twelve-mile causeway was constructed using earth and rocks which separated the Great Lake. The variation of color is due in part to the concentrations of salt, bacteria, and algae. The water north is a deep pink, reflecting high levels of saline. The water south is a cool blue due to low levels of salt. The color also changes with the seasons.

On the east shore the train began to wind through the metropolis of Salt Lake City/Ogden, Utah. The city was a welcome sight: traffic waiting at intersections, crossing alarms clanging, people walking on downtown city streets. Curious people met the gaze of their eyes as they rolled through.

Taking a cue from Percy and Grace, who were getting up and gathering their things, Barry and Bobby followed their lead. The cadence of the wheels was slowing as they had entered into a railyard with its many tracks of which new trains would be built to go to different destinations. Coming to a complete stop, Barry, Bobby, and their companions quickly climbed down the three-rung ladder to the ground.

Time and distance on the train had forged a special friendship. They shook hands and said their goodbyes. Percy and Grace enjoyed their company but were eager to find Pickles. Barry and Bobby were glad to have learned how to hop a train from Sparks, Nevada to Ogden, Utah from these two seasoned travelers. They were especially thankful to know the railyard men could be trusted, but the pair neglected to tell them a few things that could have saved them from a whole lot of trouble moving forward.

Chapter 17

JOURNEYING THROUGH
THE TUNNELS

THE BRAKEMEN, WHOSE PRIMARY FUNCTION was to break up and rebuild trains for different destinations, could tell travelers about the time of departing trains, which track they were being built on, what boxcars were good to get into, and which boxcars to avoid. Boxcars, destined to be dropped off somewhere to be loaded, could leave you out in the middle of nowhere.

Upon seeing a brakeman, Bobby approached him and asked, "Can you tell us when the next eastbound train leaves?"

The brakeman, knowing full well that hopping trains was illegal, readily responded, "The next eastbound train will be leaving shortly. You guys have a good hour and a half, and it looks like you could use the toilet and the washroom."

"That sounds like a good idea. Can you tell us where we can get a quick bite to eat?"

"Yup, there is a place down the road and it's not too expensive."

"Thanks a lot for your help."

The restroom, situated in the middle of the yard and used primarily by the brakemen, was just what Barry needed. Not quite healed from his stay in the searing sun in Reno, Barry's severely sunburned face was beginning to peel, leaving lighter and darker patches of discolored skin. Compounded by the soot and dirt, Bobby took one good look at him and said, "You look like a weathered skid row wino."

Barry's freckled Norwegian skin wasn't offering much protection against the elements. He would burn, blister, and peel. Bobby, olive-skinned, would burn, peel, and brown.

They washed the grit and dirt from their hands and faces, making them at least look presentable. Now famished, they headed for the restaurant, which was reminiscent of a school cafeteria where people would dish out the food. They knew that they had to hurry. Taking a tray, they proceeded down the line. Bobby, eyeing the array of food, said, "Man, that salad looks good!" Barry agreed and opted for a salad too.

Once they selected their food, they had to slide their trays to the cash register to pay. Well, Bobby just couldn't wait that long. Just a little bite. He pulled up the Saran Wrap covering his salad and popped a cherry tomato into his mouth. In his moment of anticipated bliss, he bit down into the tomato. The tomato burst in his mouth and a spray of tomato seeds and pulp spewed out between the gap of his front teeth and onto the crisp white smock of the guy behind the counter. In this unexpected tense, mortifying moment, Bobby, with a sheepish smile said, "Sorry, man."

The cashier was not amused. Barry found the whole scene comical. Bobby got a lecture about paying and then eating, not the other way around. With their shrunken bellies somewhat filled, they hustled back to the yard to catch the eastbound train. To this day, neither can talk about this incident without a hearty chuckle.

The guys walked to the track where the brakeman told them that an eastbound freight was being built. After walking and searching the train for suitable accommodations, and with only a few minutes to spare, they had to settle for a flat car with a load of lumber. In the middle of the load up front, Barry found a small cubbyhole made up by varying board lengths that he crawled into but was still able to poke his head up every now and then to see what was going on. The problem was it could only accommodate one person, but he opted for it because he knew it would protect him from the sun.

Unable to locate a cubbyhole similar to Barry's and running out of time, the only place Bobby could find was on the very top of the load of wood. In the center of the car was an A-frame rack. The stacked lumber leaned inward on both sides to prevent the load from falling off, left or right. About a foot above the A-frame, metal poles protruded out of the top of the load in four or five places along the top center beam. Within a few minutes the train departed. The railroad, Interstate 84, and the Weber River followed the same course heading southeast and skirting around Echo before turning northeast toward the Wasatch Mountain Range. Wasatch was established as a railroad construction camp for the continental railroad. At the time the Chinese made up a good percentage of the labor force, and the Union Pacific Railroad hired immigrant Chinese to complete the work between 1868-1869.

There were hours of long stretches of high plateau where the rails ran parallel to Interstate 84, separated by a wire fence and maybe a hundred feet of scrub. While Barry was healing in his shelter, Bobby was riding high perched atop the lumber pile, swaying in the breeze feeling like Roger Miller's "King of the Road"—acknowledging people pointing, cars honking, and kids waving. No words could fittingly describe his sense of freedom and unparalleled exuberance, an experience spawning a natural high.

Going eastbound, he continued to bask in his unique euphoria until a state trooper slowed and pulled alongside to get a better look at him. Bobby could see his mirrored shades reflecting the sun's rays as he leaned over his steering wheel gazing upward. They exchanged long glances trying to read each other's mind. Bobby gave a compulsory wave. The trooper, however, responded with a slash across his throat with his thumb. It didn't take long before the encounter was over. He mashed on the gas and was gone along with the memory of their brief contact.

About twenty-five miles out of Ogden before reaching Echo, they were about to experience their first tunnel in Weber Canyon. In all, they passed through six tunnels–some short, some long, and one that seemed to go on forever. Bobby looked past the train and could see the arch up ahead. More striking, to their left was the sight of a hard-packed clay cliff with hundreds of holes, where birds flew overhead and took up residence. The appearance and the sound of the train disrupted the birds' daily lives, but they continued to endure the chaos, knowing as soon as the train had passed, they would continue their return to normalcy until the next train presented itself.

Looming up ahead with only seconds and seeing the arch opening of the tunnel, Bobby began to worry. Bracing for the worst, Bobby vividly remembers:

> When I looked forward over the tops of the cars and engines, I could clearly see the lintel stones of the tunnel drawing closer. I was praying that my seat-of-the-pants calculations and blind trust of engineers who had designed this system of roads and tunnels had gotten it right. The thought of being swept off the top of the car against the rock face of the tunnel, Wile E. Coyote-style, was daunting. As the train approached the tunnel, I wrapped my arms around the A-frame and laid as flat as I could make myself, the ceiling less than twenty inches above me.

Then, a sigh of relief! The tunnel was only about two hundred feet. The source of dread dissipated, easing their fears about going through tunnels. Once out in the blinding sunlight, the train continued southeast toward Echo, Utah where it followed I-84. Reaching Echo, the train then took a turn northeast toward Wasatch in the direction of 1-80.

The train was climbing again up out of the plateau into rolling hills, having passed through Echo tunnel, measuring 772 feet. After a long rather taxing day, night came softly. Bobby paints a lovely picture of evening as it effortlessly eased into night.

The sun was getting low, occasionally sinking behind a hill and poking out the other side as we passed by. Not a cloud in the sky. The most beautiful blue, giving way to a firebrand sunset. I watched as the sun dipped below the horizon and was gone, dragging its glorious radiance until no evidence of it remained.

The magnificence of night dominated the heavens in the absence of city lights and city pollution. The clusters of stars were so bright, they lit up the land. The grandeur of the Milky Way manifested its brilliance in the night sky and the blanketed sun gave way once more to the cool crisp air of the high desert.

Leaving this day behind, they now lay in their sleeping bags, spirits harmonized to the rhythm of the train, and slept.

They traveled through a few more tunnels without much fanfare until they met with their nemesis. The struggling, slow-moving engines, with throttles wide open, entered the Aspen, Wyoming tunnel. The smoke from the exhaust slammed into the rock face above the arch of the tunnel, which created an evil vortex of heat and smoke that swept around them. The noise and the acrid smoke filled the tunnel to capacity.

Breathing became difficult. They wadded their shirts in a feeble attempt to filter the air. Darkness, a darkness so deep, prevented light from penetrating through the train. The incessant roar made it impossible to communicate. Their hope for a quick pass through the tunnel began to wane as the minutes and seconds dragged on. They kept asking themselves, "How long can this tunnel be?" And kept reminding themselves to "Breath slow. Breath shallow." But this strategy was to no avail as they both started coughing and choking due to the toxic diesel fumes emitted from the engines up front.

Barry fared much better having hunkered down below in the lumber pile. Being atop, Bobby, however, was fully exposed to the "hungry engines" consuming oxygen, leaving in its wake carbon dioxide as well as carbon monoxide. Impressed so strongly in the essence of his being, Bobby recalled:

My lungs burned from the smoke and mucus flowed from my eyes, nostrils, and mouth. I felt like a prisoner, entombed in a hot, dark, smoky hell, bombarded with deafening sounds that reverberated through my body, clinging to a short steel pole on top of a rail car.

Still not daring to breathe, they finally emerged from the tunnel. "Thank you, thank you, God!" was Bobby's first expression of joy. Still unable to see one another in the black shadow of night, they were at least able to acknowledge each other's existence.

"Still here?"

"Yup, still here, old friend," was Bobby's reply.

Chapter 18

YOU'RE UNDER ARREST

AROUND MIDNIGHT THE RHYTHM OF the train slowed and finally stopped at Green River, Wyoming. Barry was still in a deep sleep; Bobby, somewhat awake, was content to linger comfortably a bit longer. Without warning, frantic footsteps were now heard all over the car. Voices were shouting out. The police were climbing the woodpile searching for the guy who was standing on the lumber pile, waving at kids hours before. The state trooper must have alerted the officers before entering Weber Canyon. A flashlight beam followed the length of Bobby's sleeping bag. A voice standing over him shouted, "Got one here!"

Bobby popped his head out of the sleeping bag to see; now the flashlight beam was squarely in his eyes.

"Where are the others? Where are the others?" Raising his hand to shield his eyes, he got an unanticipated smack to his face. "I said, where are the others!?"

He stated emphatically, "There are no others. There is only me and my buddy, and he is right over there," he said, gesturing with his hand toward the front of the woodpile. Barry became the center of attention of another group of men who got him to his feet. It took some convincing for the police to believe that there were just the two of them.

They were handcuffed and put into separate police cars, along with their backpacks and sleeping bags, probably to see if their stories concurred. They were carted off to the Green River jail. Bobby's cruiser pulled up first, followed by Barry's. They were escorted into what appeared to be a newly constructed police station. A few steps inside the door sat the booking sergeant. The guys were introduced as "the ones pulled off of the train." Their handcuffs were removed.

Bobby asked, "What's going to happen to us?"

The sergeant said, "Well...the last bums we pulled off the train got thirty days. These are your backpacks, right? Empty them out, please." They did as he asked. "And now turn your pockets out."

Everything was picked through and put into separate piles. They went through Barry's and Bobby's wallets and pulled out all their contents. The officer, itemizing their belongings, made reference to Barry's duplicate license. Nothing more was said or done. Barry was greatly relieved because on his person was the illegal license of his red-haired friend, Don R. two years older than he. Phew.

After being given a written inventory of their possessions and checking for accuracy, they signed the document. The small stuff was put into safety deposit boxes. After collecting their filthy, smelly clothes, a trustee gave them a pile of new, neatly folded striped jailhouse pajamas, complete with jailhouse slippers. The trustee led them to the tiled communal shower room with a row of showerheads. And they were so happy to comply. There was hot water, soap, shampoo, and clean new towels.

Feeling rejuvenated, they were ushered to a cell that looked more like a small bedroom minus the dressers. Compared to the woodpile, they felt like they were staying at a Holiday Inn. Entering the cell through a steel door with an eight-by-twelve mesh-reinforced glass window, the trustee demonstrated the workings of the stainless-steel toilet-sink combo. No questions asked, he left.

Sitting on the twin steel beds facing the door, they took a moment to collect themselves. Barry, perplexed by the whole series of events muttered, "Why would they even search the train in the middle of the night? This makes no sense."

"It had to have been that freaking state cop who must have alerted the railroad. As soon as the train stopped, those "bastids" were all over us. They knew exactly what car we were in," Bobby railed with an edge in his voice. "Bastids."

"Stop! What are you talking about? What freaking cop?"

"Not long after we left Ogden, I was waving at the cars and the kids, and then the freakin' cop pulled up." He then proceeded to tell Barry what happened with his encounter with the cop just before entering the first tunnel.

In the morning, keys were inserted into the door and a trustee pushing a cart with breakfast trays on it said, "One for you and one for you." Lifting the domes off the plates, they found eggs, bacon, toast, home fries, and pancakes, along with orange juice and hot coffee with cream and sugar on the side.

Flabbergasted, they could not believe their good fortune—a good night's sleep on a real mattress with clean sheets, fluffy pillows, a new wool blanket, and a hearty breakfast, something they had not enjoyed since leaving Poulsbo, Washington. And it definitely didn't mirror their first jailhouse experiences a month before.

When the trustee came back to collect the trays and empty plates, he said with a playful grin, "It looks like they're gonna let you guys go. I'll go get your stuff so you can get dressed." He left and returned in less than five minutes, wheeling in a cart with all their clothes. Even their dirty spare clothes stashed in the back packs were washed and folded. Both were now dumbfounded, and they just had to ask him why they were being treated so well.

"This is a brand-new facility. For the past week the staff has been running through drills on how to run the place, from food prep to sanitation and all other areas of service. You fellas are our very first customers in this brand-new jail."

Again, one has to ask how lucky they can be?

Dressed in their freshly laundered clothes, they waited patiently in their cell until the doors opened. A cop not seen before motioned them out. "Over there please." Meanwhile, another desk sergeant retrieved their safety deposit boxes. Once their inventory was checked out and the document was signed, they were good to go.

Confused, Bobby asked the desk sergeant, "We were told last night that the last bums pulled off the train got thirty days."

Taking off his glasses as if to get a better look, the sergeant said, "Yeah, that's right. But for some reason the Union Pacific Railroad decided not to prosecute, so...you're free to go. You two wait right there for a few minutes. The chief is going to give you a ride to the bus station."

The chief of the police department was a sizable middle-aged man with a well-toned and muscular physique. He wore a white shirt adorned with his rank insignia, name tag, and pins. On his shoulder was the proud department's patch. On the opposite shoulder was the American flag. A sharp crease ran down his pant legs ending with polished black shoes. They sensed no malice as he walked toward them. They figured he might have been briefed in advance of the situation and had already mapped out a plan on how he was to deal with them. Considering their treatment thus far, they felt at ease, with just a touch of apprehension. The chief approached them with an air of authority that everybody in the room recognized.

"Good morning. I am the Green River chief of police. You are free to go. But remember it is illegal to hitchhike in the state and you can't hop trains, so I am taking you to the Greyhound bus station and I highly recommend you take the bus to Colorado. Now, gather up your stuff and follow me, please. Let's go."

In the midmorning air, they followed him to his car. They sat in the back seat with their backpacks. After they had pulled away from the police station, the chief began to reiterate his stance.

"You know, it's unusual that the railroad chose not to prosecute you guys. The standard is thirty days." Making eye contact with them in the rearview mirror, he continued in a stern voice, "You two are very lucky, very lucky."

They pulled into the bus station. He put the car in park, so they thought it was the end of their jailhouse chapter. But then the officer turned off the ignition and stepped out as they were doing the same. He walked with them all the way to the ticket counter and stood behind them as the guys inquired as to the cost of two tickets to Colorado. The chief was satisfied, a trip to the bus station with final admonishments complete. Job done! The chief walked away with confidence, never uttering a goodbye. He walked back to his car and drove away.

The man at the counter said, "That'll be $2.50 each."

Barry and Bobby looked at each other and walked away from the counter trying to decide what to do. Bobby was the first to say, "I'm not spending $2.50 on a bus ticket."

"Bobby, it doesn't make any sense to go to Colorado and be in the same situation that we're already in. Let's get outta here," were Barry's final words.

They knew the risks of hitchhiking in Wyoming and Colorado, so they had to maintain a low profile. For Bobby, it was a high-stakes gamble to hitchhike. His concern about getting arrested and ending up in jail made him overly cautious. For Barry, it was slim to none that police would be looking for hitchhikers out of the city limits. If they could not take the bus, then the only alternative was to start walking and see what happened.

So they left the bus station and started walking toward the east side of town. They made it through the business district and were now approaching the city limit. Buildings were getting few and far between, and then there were none. There was only the U.S. highway ahead of them, a prairie desert, and the mountains off in the distance. To the right was the railyard where the guys were dragged out the day before.

They realized walking around in the railyard could draw suspicion. No doubt, the railyard workers were aware two guys got hauled off the train the night before and those two guys were back. The Union Pacific might not be so lenient a second time, so they walked. Paranoia eased its way into their psyche. Each time they heard a car, they would turn their head to look to determine if it was a police car. As soon as the threat (real or imagined) dissipated, they would casually stick out their thumbs. Nobody was stopping.

They agreed this was going to be a rough patch to traverse. After some time in the fierce intensity of the sun, they decided it was unnecessary and unwise to continue walking. The next center of population was a hefty distance away. As they patiently waited for a ride, a duo off in the distance was walking toward them on the other side of the highway. They greeted each other with a friendly hello and a wave before crossing the road.

The two guys began to tell Barry and Bobby a tale of their experience the night before. It seemed that they had been abducted by a group of cowboys who had abused and terrorized them all night long. Apparently, it was some sort of annual hazing event where the cowboys would run the hippies out of town. They said that there was gunplay involved as well. They were clearly shaken as they told their story.

After Barry and Bobby shared their story about landing in jail, they went their separate ways. The duo continued down the road into town, while Barry and Bobby continued their vigil on the side of the road, hoping for a ride out of town. Things weren't looking good, but it was still early in the day. The worst-case scenario would be to find a place to sleep by the side of the road and pick up where they left off in the morning.

Chapter 19

A NEAR FATALITY AND EASING THE PAIN IN AN EL CAMINO

SUDDENLY, OFF TO THE RIGHT, the sound of the loud familiar crash of heavy metal colliding burst, the peristaltic wave. In Bobby's own words:

> *From the epicenter of the source, the wave it created spread 360 degrees in all directions. The arc of the expanding sound wave impacted us and sped away at 760 miles per hour, chaotically impacting objects and returned to them, defused, as echoes.*

The train! They recognized it simultaneously. It now was the moment to act. There was no railyard, and the train was moving slowly, so for them this was a no-brainer. They quickly gathered up their backpacks and took off running. The train was groaning and squealing and slowly coming to life with the engines whining and booming. They hurriedly ran down a grassy embankment, where at the bottom lay a cattail marsh, perhaps twenty feet across. Slogging through muck, they could feel the sensation of the heavy mud making a failed attempt to suck the boots from their feet. They stumbled up on the other side of the marsh, fighting not to fall face first. Exhausted but energized, with arms flailing to maintain balance, they emerged from the muck and the water victorious. They sprinted to the train.

A parade of unloaded flat cars was all that was offered. There was no time for contemplation as the train was picking up speed. Bobby was running in the lead alongside a flat car. Barry was right behind him. On the fly, they shifted their packs from the back to the front of their bodies, which enabled them to toss their packs onto the flatbed. As the three-rung ladder at the end of the car approached, Bobby reached out and grabbed hold of it, as he swung his feet onto the bottom rung. He was up and on.

Even though he hurried to clear the ladder, Barry had lost momentum while the pace of the train had accelerated. When he grabbed for the ladder rung, it was jerked from his grasp. He was flung into the crushed granite of the roadbed with the wheels of the charging train a few feet away. Even to this day, Barry has nightmares about losing his legs during his ordeal. It took Bobby a few moments to realize that Barry had fallen and had never made it on the train. The shock that Barry might not make it on board made him break into a cold sweat.

Oh my God. I contemplated that if his efforts to get on board failed, the only aid that I could offer would be to throw his backpack from the train where he could retrieve it. The train was moving way too fast for me to get off.

Meanwhile, scrambling to his feet, Barry raced to catch the ladder of several flatbeds behind. Barry's dogged grit, athletic ability, and pure adrenaline saved him despite his unhealed cracked toe and bloody palms resulting from his fall onto the sharp traprock. Now running solo, he was determined to get on the train to retrieve his backpack. He wasn't going anywhere without it.

Barry was finally able to gain momentum and was only three flatbeds behind before he was able to grab on to the ladder, feet momentarily dragging until he could reach the next rung. He made it!

Bobby riding three cars forward watched the scene unfold. He could no longer make out Barry's facial features. His fair skin was now very red. His head jerked from side to side as he furiously pumped his arms and legs. Bobby lost sight of him below the deck of the car, but his gaze was welded to the spot where Barry had slipped away from his sight. Seconds passed. Bobby described it as "Barry rising up like a battered phoenix over the side of the car."

Against the odds, bruised physically and mentally, Barry survived. The train was now up to speed and hammering along. They had escaped the pitfalls of Green River.

Exhausted and totally spent, it took a few minutes for Barry to collect himself. As the reader might conclude, Barry is a man of few words, but when asked about how he felt at the time, he responded:

I knew everything came down to grabbing the ladder. The speed of the train made the challenge more daunting but grabbing that ladder and pulling myself up was all that consumed me.

After a few minutes to recoup, Barry sat up and turned to face Bobby, who waved a solemn greeting. Barry held up his left hand and pointed to his bloodied palm with his other hand and Bobby then realized that he had been injured during the fall.

Still running high on adrenaline, Barry's fears never interfered with what he knew he had to do: one, get to Bobby and two, retrieve his backpack. Calculating the cars were not more than four feet apart and never doubting that he could easily make it, he took a few steps back, ran forward, and leaped over the gap between the cars. He did this twice to get to where Bobby was sitting.

"Damn it! Barry, I wouldn't do that shit. You trying to get yourself killed?"

Barry and Bobby lingered to regain their composure. The two of them just sat in stony silence smack-dab in the middle of a flat car in plain view. They both now realized they needed to find cover. A couple of cars forward to where they were standing was an automobile carrier, loaded with brand-new cars. The only obstacle was they had to jump the gaps between the cars.

Barry looked at his friend intently, and said, "Bobby, sitting out in the open is not good. I did it; you can do it. Watch." Barry threw his backpack onto the next car first and then jumped the gap and coaxed Bobby to make the leap of faith. After throwing his own backpack, Bobby jumped and thought, *Not so bad.*

Walking to the front of the flatbed, they inspected the auto carrier and saw that it was similar to what they had previously done. One more jump and they were on the auto hauler. The car was loaded with factory fresh Chevrolet El Caminos. Sweet. They climbed up to the top level and selected the most forward car. They put their packs in the pickup truck-style bed of the El Camino and jumped in being as inconspicuous as possible.

Bobby looked at Barry. "Not bad. Nice soft ride, huh?"

Laying in the back, Barry wondered aloud, "Wouldn't it be cool if the doors were unlocked?"

Bobby said, "Give it a try."

Barry turned on his knees, reached around the side of the car, grasped the door handle, pushed the button with his thumb, and *pop!* Once again, they were struck by the magic of Lady Luck.

Leaving their backpacks safely stored in the back, they stealthily slid out of the back making their way to the front, Bobby in the driver's seat and Barry on the passenger's side. Climbing out of the bed and into the cab, their first thought was, *Oh, the smell of a new car.*

Barry settled in and faced Bobby. "Is this seat back as far as it will go?"

Bobby reached down and pulled the adjustment level. Much

to their delight the seat slid back allowing for plenty of leg room.

"This is great!"

"It's hot in here," said Barry. "Let's roll the window down."

"Damn, Barry! Look at this view!

Unbelievable. The two guys ridin' in style on the top of an auto hauler in a brand-new Chevy El Camino! Can anybody else make this claim? They were outliers. Jumping the gaps paid off in spades! In a few hours their good fortune would come to an end when the train stopped in the vicinity of Sinclair, Wyoming.

Chapter 20

STOPPED, STRANDED, STRESSED

THE TRAIN HAD SLOWED TO a stop, not unusual. Their first thought was maybe the train stopped on a sidetrack to allow another train to pass as it was going west in the opposite direction. They were not too concerned. Suddenly, with a lurch, the train began to move forward followed by an abrupt stop. With a jerk the train began to move into reverse.

Bobby, who was still in the driver's seat, looked off to the right and with an element of surprise in his voice said, "Hey, Barry! That looks like our train over there!"

Sure enough, they could hear the engine moving away. Quickly, they got out of the Chevy to investigate the commotion. To their dismay they found themselves sitting on a sidetrack with a few other cars. There was one final clunk before the engines rehooked themselves to the main train, leaving the two of them stranded!

They were dumped off in the middle of nowhere, prairie all around. There was something that looked like a town way off a couple of miles away to the west. They questioned if it could have been a mirage but then decided it had to be a town and began to walk. The soft ground under their feet made walking a bit more laborious, sinking in a little with each step. There were patches of low-growing scrub that they had to weave around occasionally.

The town seemed to grow in size as they got nearer. It was not much of a town. In hindsight, the town might have been in Sinclair, Wyoming. On the west side of the main street there was a gas station market, a laundromat, and other essential stores. The east side of town showed signs of an impoverished community living a hand to mouth existence. There were rows of weathered mobile homes, time-worn playthings scattered here and there, and a few people roaming around. With nothing more to see, there was no reason to stay.

It was still midday when they began walking toward Interstate 80 less than a half mile south of the town. With no trains to hop, the guys decided to hitchhike even though a ride didn't look too promising. As they crossed the overpass of the interstate nearing the entrance/exit ramp, a "'61 two-tone dark blue four-door Chevy" was exiting the highway. A dark-skinned muscular man sporting a black handlebar mustache leaned out of the driver's side window to holler, "Which way you headed?" as he slowly passed by. "East," was their reply. There was an occupant in the passenger seat. "We're headed to get some gas. Wait here and we'll be back to get you."

Bobby looked at Barry, and said, "That was quick."

"Yeah, that was weird. Nobody ever did that before. We weren't even hitchhiking."

They decided to head toward the ramp to hitchhike. If someone did stop, fine. If not, they had nothing to lose, no time wasted. Surprisingly, they saw the '61 Chevy getting on the ramp heading east. True to their word, they stopped. The driver stepped out of the car to open the trunk where the guys threw their backpacks in while his buddy stood by watching. The cowboys wore Wrangler jeans with well-worn cowboy boots. Their Stetson hats were arranged side by side in the back window.

Standing by the car, the driver asked, "Where are you guys going?"

"We're headed east to Massachusetts."

"Well...if you agree to buy a tank of gas, you can ride with us for as far as that tank of gas will take us. After that...you're on your own.

They agreed with no discussion. For Barry the deal didn't sit well. Hitchhiking and paying for gas made no sense. Bobby was down to his last five dollars. Paying for gas would leave them not only penniless but stranded.

They introduced themselves. "I'm Bobby and this is my buddy, Barry."

"I'm Ino. The name's Hawaiian." (Ino means storm and can have a terrifying or ominous meaning.) Pointing to the man sitting beside him he said, "This is Cole."

Ino and Cole told them that they had just sold their spare tire to buy some gas. They told them that they were rodeo riders who were following the circuit of rodeo events. Ino rode bulls. Cole didn't talk much and never disclosed what he did at the rodeo. To bolster their income, they would seek out artifacts, such as arrowheads and geodes. During a side trip to a ghost town, they showed Barry and Bobby some previously collected examples of geodes they had stored in the trunk. The cowboys would also collect prickly pear cacti that they would uproot and then pack into the mineral halves to make it easier for transport. They had a market for this stuff somewhere.

Bobby, being a motorhead of sorts, took an interest in Ino's car. It was a "'61 four-door Chevy Biscayne." What made it somewhat unusual was it had a high performance 348 big block engine (the precursor to the famed engine 409 immortalized by the Beach Boys' song in '62). Its high performance came with a price in that it was a gas guzzler. Bobby suspected that the car might have been a police car. The telltale was that it was a base model car, with a big motor, a spotlight on the door, and was painted two-tone dark blue.

Riding along, Ino asked, "Do either of you have a knife or a gun?" After hesitating he continued, "Because if you do, we could eat rabbit tonight. I can blind a jackrabbit with my spotlight"—pointing to the spotlight on the door— "and throw the knife or shoot a rabbit."

Bobby was quick to answer, "Nope, no knife, no gun."

Barry, ever so cautious, remained silent. It wasn't until later that he remembered he had a scout knife somewhere in his backpack.

When they got to Cheyenne, Barry paid for the gas and Bobby went into the convenience store to buy a loaf of bread and a package of bologna. He was now becoming more uncomfortable in their presence. So much so, he committed the tag number to memory, Oregon BYC..., by associating the letters with the word *bicycle*. As they drove back onto the interstate, Bobby made everyone a bologna sandwich even though it was not part of the deal to feed them. Ino however, was not satisfied with just one.

Turning around to face Bobby, he said, "Hey, give me another sandwich."

Bobby responded with a flat, "No."

Bobby's terse "No" created an awkward silence and like the song sung by the Four Seasons... "it wasn't golden." Barry was thinking that he probably would have given Ino the second bologna sandwich if it was his to give, but it wasn't. Barry was silent as Bobby began to explain his reasoning to Ino. "Ino, Barry and I are gonna need what's left for ourselves after you drop us off."

Bobby was expecting to part ways with these guys when the car needed to be refueled again in about two hundred miles or four hours, but Barry thought differently. He believed they were being sucked into a quagmire and was not sure where it was going to lead them. He didn't have enough money to keep filling up their gas tank.

There was an incremental subtle tension building as they were driving along. Having ridden eastward through a fair portion of Wyoming, they entered Nebraska. Conversation subsided as night revealed itself. Ino announced that he would have to find some place to relieve himself. A short time later, he turned off onto a dirt road running perpendicular and south to the highway. Close to the highway, there was a cattle grate to cross.

After about a mile, Barry was more than concerned and asked, "Why are we going so far?"

Ino replied, "I need to take a dump. This is as good a place as any."

If there had been any doubt about any shenanigans that might be in the making, it was gone. Barry thought, *Something bad is going down.* And he was hoping Bobby felt the same. But before Barry could say anything more, Ino pulled off from the main dirt road about 150 feet from where other vehicles had left their tracks.

The car stopped. Ino and Cole got out of the car and opened the rear doors allowing Barry and Bobby to get out. Neither of the side doors had any interior handles so the only way they could get out was either by rolling down the windows or having someone open the doors from the outside. Hmm. They all separated to pee in private.

Barry, still thinking something wasn't right, walked approximately seventy-five feet into the darkness but remained close enough to see Ino grab a roll of toilet paper from the opened trunk, illuminated by its dim light. Barry remained watching Ino as he walked into the pitch of night. Bobby had returned to the back seat of the car. Cole was positioned close to the front passenger side door. Barry remained watchful. His attention wasn't so much on Cole; he was more concerned with Ino, who walked back to the car, toilet paper in hand, and leaned into the back seat where Bobby was sitting. *Something just isn't right* echoed in Barry's head and there was no way he could communicate this to his friend.

This became a pivotal moment for both Barry and Bobby. As Bobby sat in the car waiting, Ino feigned with his right hand he was going to store the toilet paper under the driver's seat. Within seconds he retracted his arm, shifted slightly, and dropped his full body weight on Bobby, forcing him down onto the rear seat in a prone position on his back. The hand that held the toilet paper moments earlier, now held a knife, the point pressed against the side of his neck. Bobby, who was in a compromised position, made a feeble attempt to wriggle free but Ino was much too heavy and much too strong.

Meanwhile, Barry, still enveloped in darkness, was unaware of what was actually going down until Bobby was dragged from the back seat of the car to his feet. Standing in stillness, listening to the untamed thumping of his heart as adrenaline coursed through his body, Barry saw Ino behind Bobby with a knife on his throat.

Barry's fears were realized the moment Ino bellowed, "Barry, come out from wherever you are, or I will slit your friend's throat. Then, when I'm done, I'll hunt you down!"

It never occurred to Barry to fear for his own life. He was seventy-five feet away, was safely cocooned in pitch-blackness, and was a good runner, even with his cracked toe. However, with the apprehension of Bobby, the narrative changed. It was no longer a lighthearted story about two friends traversing through Canada and the U.S. Instead, at this juncture of their journey, Barry found himself in a literal life-or-death situation. If he did not comply, his friend might be killed. If he obeyed there was at least a chance both could survive the ordeal. He decided to walk out of the dark toward the car.

"Come...closer...closer," Ino repeated as he continued to draw Barry in. Reluctantly, he walked into the light of the open trunk and doors.

Holding Bobby hostage with his knife to his throat, Ino looked at Barry and ordered, "Take off all your clothes." Pointing, he said, "and put them there." With a stern gruff voice and unflinching eyes, he added, "Give me that watch." As Barry was stripping down, Cole was collecting his clothes, searching through them to find any money or valuables. He meticulously went through each pile, turning out socks, shaking out boots, and checking to see if either had a money belt.

Once within reach, Ino transferred his assault from Bobby to Barry. He now had the knife to Barry's throat. He ordered Bobby to strip naked, go to the front left corner of the car, and in a menacing voice said, "Face away, don't you turn around, and don't you run!"

Ino then turned to Barry who was standing by the left taillight. As he tried to get Barry down, Barry's reflexes kicked in and he resisted by shifting his weight. There was a tussle and Ino finally wrestled Barry to the ground with the knife still positioned to his throat, making a shallow cut. With the sound of the scuffle Bobby feared Barry was being stabbed to death, and if that was the case, the only thing to do was save himself. Ino was now preoccupied with tying Barry's wrists together behind his back, using Barry's own belt.

Instinctively, Bobby turned and met Barry's gaze. "Bobby, I'm okay."

In a turn of events, Barry's life now depended upon Bobby not running. Bobby froze in place. The sound of Barry calling out to Bobby turned Ino's focus on Bobby who had broken Ino's command.

He turned to look at Bobby with a penetrating gaze and in a threatening manner said, "I told you not to turn around. Come over here"—pointing a finger— "now!"

As Bobby approached him, he straightened to face Bobby, who recalled "seeing a flash of white as I was punched, landing on the ground beside Barry."

Cole stopped what he was doing to watch while Barry and Bobby squirmed on their sides, trying to regain their equilibrium in order to get into a sitting position.

Ino had worked himself up in the persona of a madman. Seared in his memory, Bobby recalls:

Ino, standing over us, looked deranged with his mouth pulled back tight, exposing his gritted teeth. He held the knife in his clenched hand in a menacing manner. His eyes, wild. His breathing, heavy. Seething with rage! Pure hatred hovered above us.

As the dwindling spark of hope extinguished, in that moment of despair, it was reignited with a flicker of lights. In the distance came headlights. In an instant, Ino's spell was broken. The maniacal expression on his face was replaced with nervous concern. He was clearly shaken by this turn of events, his eyes darting around, briefly meeting the eyes of Cole. One could speculate all Ino was thinking about was the unexpected intrusion of a witness, who could change the course of his devious plan.

Barry and Bobby knew the situation could still end very badly for them but reflecting upon this moment, they knew a small victory was given to them. For Bobby, it was "a gift, from the beating wings of a butterfly. The Angel of Death had passed over us."

Ino immediately bent down, grabbed Barry by the hair and pulled him up to his feet. Still tied, he threw him headlong into the passenger front seat and slammed the door.

While racing around to the front of the car to get to the driver's seat, he looked at Bobby and bellowed, "Gather up your shit and get in the car."

Shifting his eyes toward Cole, he commanded, "Quick! throw their backpacks into the trunk."

A truck was rattling down the washboard road surface. As the old Chevy truck neared, Ino slid toward Barry and pulled him closer to him, purposely making them appear like a couple parking all the while keeping the knife to his throat.

Bobby had gathered an armful of his and Barry's belongings. Seeing shirts and boots, Bobby had to make a second effort to collect the rest of the items strewn about. The old pickup truck slowed, and the driver took a good long look at the situation. They sat and waited for the truck to disappear north over the horizon in the direction of the interstate.

Once the truck went by and the threat passed Ino untied Barry; he ordered him to get into the back seat with Bobby.

Cole returned to the front seat. "You guys can get dressed."

In the ensuing melee of sorting out their clothing, and putting them back on, Bobby failed to find his underpants, so he had to pull on his pants without them. Ino and Cole began to talk among themselves.

"Cole, did you find any money?"

"Just a couple of wadded dollar bills and a handful of nickels from Bobby. The only thing I found on Barry was four dollars and thirty dollars' worth of traveler's checks."

"You"—pointing to Bobby— "get in the front seat. Just climb over. Cole, get in the back."

In the meantime, Barry slid over behind Ino to make room for Cole to get into the rear passenger seat. Ino started the car and began driving back toward the Interstate.

The travelers' checks were the only thing of real value. While driving, the wheels in Ino's mind were turning, he was devising a plan to extract those monies to his benefit. After riding what seemed like hours, Ino began to berate Bobby for not giving him a second sandwich earlier in the day.

"This shit is mine now. Do you want a sandwich, asshole?"

Bobby told him, "Yes, I do."

In a condescending voice, he replied, "Well, you're not getting one." It goes without saying he did not like Bobby.

He exited the highway north onto a secondary road that ran perpendicular to the interstate and into the outskirts of some little highway town, probably Ogallala.

Approaching a gas station, Ino yelled, "Cole, get me my Stetson."

He grabbed the hat from Cole's hand, placed it on Bobby's head and tipped it down over his eyes.

"Close your eyes and pretend you're asleep."

In his right hand he held the knife that he pressed into Bobby's side above his hip. A rag or some sort of covering was used as a shield to hide his hand with the knife.

"And Barry, don't do anything stupid if you like your friend."

With that, they drove to the gas station and rolled up to the pump. He told the attendant to "fill 'er up" and to check the oil.

When it came time to pay, he turned to face Barry, saying, "Here you need to sign these. Oh, and while you're at it, why don't you cash the rest of them."

Barry unquestioningly signed his name. The balance in cash was given in return, which Ino took. They pulled out of the gas station and headed back to the interstate. They drove for some time before Bobby was ordered to climb back into the rear passenger seat with Barry, Cole regained his seat in the front. A discussion between Ino and Cole was now taking place as to what they were to do with the guys.

"Well, Cole, what do we do with these guys now? I say kill 'em."

Before Cole could answer, Barry piped in, "What, are you kidding me? You're going to kill us for thirty-four fucking dollars? It doesn't make any sense. Thirty-four bucks. I can't believe you're talking about killing us for thirty-four dollars!"

Bobby chimed in, "Just let us out. We won't say a word."

"Shut the fuck up!"

There was an uncomfortable silence. However, a private conversation between Ino and Cole was taking place in low whispers.

Not being privy to their mumbled exchange, Barry and Bobby speculated they were discussing their fate. After riding for about an hour, the long silence was broken when Ino pulled off to the side of the road into the breakdown lane of I-80. Just before stopping, Cole's hand found its way between the interior wall of the car and into the passenger compartment where Bobby sat. Between his fingers was a dollar bill. He waved it slightly to get his attention, clearly wanting him to have it. Bobby timidly took it from him, somewhat suspicious of his motive. Being so close to freedom, he didn't want to jeopardize the situation. Leary of taking the dollar and Ino maybe finding out, they could be left for dead on the side of the road. He took a deep breath, wadded up the dollar bill, and placed it under the seat in front of him.

"Look, I'm gonna let you go. I have your identities and I know where you live. If you report us, we will hunt you down and we will kill you or we will find someone who will."

In exchange for their freedom, they made a solemn promise not to take any action against them. A promise kept. Convinced of their sincerity, the doors were opened. Barry and Bobby stepped out into the desolate, cold, Nebraska night.

Ino opened the trunk of the car and brought out their backpacks. Looking from the backpacks to the guys, he emphatically asked, "If I do a thorough search of your backpacks, I won't find anything of value, right?"

Barry said, "You have everything man. The only thing might be the jar of peanut butter and jelly."

Without hesitation, Ino opened Barry's backpack and grabbed the jar. He asked Barry if there was anything that he had confiscated from him that he wanted back.

Barry said, "Yeah. I would like my watch back. My mom gave it to me when I graduated from high school." Surprisingly, Ino gave it to him.

Then Ino said, "By the way, there's a rest area about a mile up the road."

The dollar Cole had given Bobby, the one stashed under his seat, was still on Bobby's mind.

Before letting them loose, Bobby spoke up and said, "My underwear is in the car somewhere, I'd like to get it."

Ino agreed. He leaned into the back seat, found the underwear, and continued a short search for the dollar. He found it where he had deposited it moments before. He took the dollar and wadded it up in his underwear. It was a big gamble. No telling what would have happened if Ino thought Bobby was holding out. Bobby's gamble paid off. Ino had no interest in handling Bobby's funky underwear.

The two thieves loaded up and drove off into the night, waiting for some distance to pass before turning the headlights on. One could surmise it was a last-ditch effort to keep them from reading the tag number as they drove off. But Bobby had already committed the number to memory. Oregon tag number BYC...

They stood and watched as the '61 Chevy drove away. Their immediate concern was that Ino and Cole might change their mind and come back. Barry and Bobby hurriedly exited the spot where they stood and headed out into the prairie. They walked about a hundred feet and then paralleled the highway. It was about two or three in the morning so there was very little traffic. With every passing car, they would crouch down to keep a low profile. Every car was suspect with thoughts of *it could be them*. Trudging in the prairie scrub was labor intensive, but they kept up the pace, knowing it was better to walk in the cool of night than in the heat of the day.

After about an hour of slowly navigating through the scrub and ducking every car that went by, they could see a glow on the horizon. They kept walking. Drawing closer, they could see the glow was a rest area alongside the interstate in the proximity of Brady, Nebraska. There were some cars and a few semis parked. After scanning the lot for Ino's car, they walked over to the service building that housed restrooms and a few vending machines. They went into the men's room seeking shelter from the cold. As soon as Barry and Bobby stepped through the door a few of the travelers, who were already rolled out, raised their heads. Initially, they cast a wary eye, but after a brief greeting and small talk to set them at ease, the guys shared what had transpired hours before.

As soon as they left the confines of the restroom at daybreak, Bobby dug into his pants pocket and retrieved the one-dollar bill Cole had passed to him. Indebted for the small gift, he went to the vending machine and bought a twin pack of Reese's peanut butter cups. With his share of the dollar, Barry, who had not had a smoke since the day before, bought a pack of cigarettes, not just any brand of cigarettes, but a pack of Kools. They walked over to the nearest picnic table and sat down spent, the mood somber. Bobby opened his twin pack of Reese's peanut butter cups, handing one to Barry. Likewise, Barry opened his pack of Kools, giving one to Bobby. As they enjoyed their small pleasures, they rehashed and analyzed the turn of events that had unfolded during a twelve-hour period. They were drained of emotions, but still on high alert. They described it as "battle fatigue." They had just experienced the battle for their lives trying to talk Ino out of killing them.

Chapter 21

TRUDGING FORWARD IN FEAR

As ONE WOULD EXPECT, NAVIGATING toward home would be a challenging and precarious undertaking. They learned early on that it was illegal to hitchhike on any interstate. Now, with no money, they could find themselves in jail for vagrancy. But their minds were made up; they were committed to getting home. While walking through the parking lot toward the on-ramp of the interstate, a step side Chevy pickup truck, pulling a small weathered trailer, caught Bobby's attention. They inched closer to the truck and spotted a man, his wife, and two children. Making eye contact, the man greeted them with a "good morning." A conversation ensued.

Whether it was Barry or Bobby, one of them related their story of the previous day and how they felt safer hopping trains. After listening intently, the man told them he was a truck driver, who months ago, had been involved in a serious wreck. He had suffered a life-threatening injury and was at a point in his recovery where he was able to be up and about. It was apparent his body would take time to heal. He was bent when he walked and kept his arm close to his body. He told them he and his family were on their way to visit relatives in Lincoln.

During their conversation, the older man reckoned these two

guys were in a bad way and certainly would do no harm. After a moment of contemplation, he extended an invitation to ride along with him. He explained that space was limited and the younger of his two children had to sit on his mama's lap. He didn't have much to offer, but if they were willing, they could ride in the trailer. Realizing Barry and Bobby had not eaten since noon the day before and knowing one peanut butter cup each could not sustain them, he offered them a can of potatoes from among the family's rations. They readily accepted.

Walking the guys to the trailer and handing them a can opener, he made his way back to the pickup truck, started the engine, and drove off. It was a typical trailer. They sat opposite one another at a jutted table, which could easily be converted into a bed for the family. Barry and Bobby, famished, immediately opened the can of potatoes, savoring each and every bite. Never in Barry's life had he eaten canned potatoes. Even to this day he says, "They were the best potatoes I ever ate."

They rode for about two hundred miles from Brady to Lincoln, Nebraska. Worn-out and extremely fatigued, they slept for the duration of the ride and were awakened when the old truck pulled over to the side of the road. Once stopped, they heard a knock on the door before it opened.

The man looked at them and smiled. "This looks as good a place as any." Pointing south he went on to say, "The train yard is over there."

After their brief goodbyes and expression of thanks, he wished them well before driving off to see his kin.

With the memory of the events just prior, Barry and Bobby had come to the conclusion traveling by rail was much safer than hitchhiking. Lincoln had a sizable yard, a hump yard, so it wasn't hard to find. Insights gleaned from past ventures through railyards prompted them to walk inconspicuously, fearing another trip to jail.

Bobby walked over to the brakeman and said, "Hi."

The brakeman looked at him without any trace of concern or suspicion. "Hi, what can I do for ya?"

"I'm looking for an eastbound train."

The brakeman said, "Whatever you do, don't get into any of the cars over there"—pointing to the left—"Those cars are going over the hump. An 'eastbound' is being built on track three." He looked at his watch, and continued, "and is scheduled to be leaving soon."

Bobby smiled and said, "Thanks for the tip."

There were a few open boxcars to choose from, one already occupied. They looked at each other, quickly deciding to check it out. Two fellow travelers sat inside the doorway, one with his legs dangling down and the other with his legs drawn up with his arms wrapped around his knees. Still vulnerable and guarded, they greeted each other.

The first man introduced himself. John was warm and engaging. He was not a tall man, about five-foot-eight or so. He had piercing blue eyes. The couple of days of stubble on his face was framed by longish light brown hair. His clothes were old but not dirty. When he spoke, he had an air of intelligence about him. John introduced his companion whose name was Franklin. Conversely, he was a nappy fellow, not so well-kept. He was considerably taller than his traveling mate, maybe six feet. He was dirty and wore filthy clothes. His close-cropped hair looked as though it had been cut with a kitchen knife. He appeared strange, making the guys a bit leery.

The yard was a hump yard, in that, in the process of breaking and building trains, a switcher engine would push a row of cars up an incline (the hump), and when a car reached the top, a brakeman would pull the lever to unhook the car from the rest and allow the car to freely roll on its own down the hill. While rolling down the hill it would pass a switcher tower where a man would direct the rolling car onto one of a number of tracks. On each of these tracks were trains being built to be sent in different directions. This is a very noisy process. When the rolling car meets up with the car it is to be coupled with, there is a collision and the resulting noise generated is beyond deafening. This process goes on in rapid succession all day long.

John was open to them, and they became comfortable in his presence. From their brief conversation, they knew he was heading east. They asked if he minded if they shared the boxcar with them. John replied, "Sure, hop on."

John and his travel mate, who didn't seem like they were well-suited companions, had already claimed the back end where all their stuff was stored; Barry and Bobby, out of caution, settled to the front, separated by fifty feet of floor. The boxcar was quite clean. There was some dunnage, bits of cardboard and stuff, left over from the previous load. It looked like the floor might have been swept recently. Barry and Bobby sat and kept tabs on their two buddies from a distance. They agreed the pair was definitely a study in contrasts. John was a healthy and fit man of about fifty years old. He emanated a quality of confidence in and control of himself. He didn't seem to be a drinker and was more of a long-term thinker. His tan canvas pack was well organized and well cared for. He took care of himself and his stuff.

His partner, on the other hand, was an unknown quantity, giving them no clues to his demeanor. His motions weren't fluid and were somewhat awkward, even jerky at times. He was quiet and aloof. He would watch his newfound travelers with eagle eyes. His suspicion aroused their own apprehension and vigilance while in his presence. They often thought that if they were standing or sitting in the open doorway, it would be a simple task for him to give them a push or kick them in the back, and out the door they'd go. They were cordial to him but did not engage.

After a while Barry and Bobby went over to formally meet their traveling companions and to swap stories. From their recollections, John seemed to take an interest and enjoyed their company. Dubbed the "Refined Hobo" he told them that he was on his annual trip from Washington State to Florida to see his daughter, and that he had made this trip more than a few times in the past. He traveled the same route every year, making the same stops along the way. This leg of the trip would see him into Cicero, Illinois, just outside Chicago, then into Chicago to the Salvation Army Mission, where he planned to get food, a shower, and shelter for the night before moving on. He was well versed, well-spoken, and he knew his way around. Just like with Percy and Grace, his wisdom was well received.

Seeking rest, the dunnage proved to be valuable in making makeshift mattresses to sleep on. The train raced through eastern Nebraska, into Iowa, and on to Illinois. There were miles and miles of cornfields and golden grains. Intermittently, one could see houses and barns. The train slowed to slip through small farming towns to the sound of clanging bells at crossroads and waiting cars. Passing small, dilapidated communities on "the other side of the tracks," people would look up, catching a fleeting glance as they rolled by. Bobby made sure he did not engage.

With Franklin dozing over in the far corner of his end of the boxcar, Barry, Bobby, and John took up residence in the open doorway, watching the scene pass by. Barry was suddenly alerted to something outside the speeding train. He was looking intently and excitedly shouted, "Bobby, Bobby," without taking a breath in between, "that's pot! It's all over the place, look!" Without a doubt, Barry knew his pot, having grown it since high school. The pot was so thick and lush it formed a barrier between the train and whatever was growing on the other side. There were miles and miles of it. The plants were huge, about six feet tall leaning toward the train, but just out of reach. They were healthy-looking but had no buds. In WWII it was known as hemp.

Barry, who was out of cigarettes, devised a plan. The plan was for Bobby to hold the back of his belt and for John to hold Bobby's belt, which allowed Barry to extend his whole body all the way out to grab branches of pot. Meanwhile, Franklin was passively watching wide-eyed as they executed their plan. One could only imagine what would have happened if anyone had let go.

They ended up with a decent pile of pot. Bobby took out the Sterno stove from his backpack and the sheets of aluminum foil that they had folded into squares for transport. Bobby took the foil and shaped it into a bowl, while Barry pulled off the leaves. The stripped leaves were then placed in the bowl that was positioned over a Sterno stove for a bit. Voilà, badly dried pot! Barry pulled out his Top rolling papers, rolled up some joints, and they were in business!

John had told them that he had never smoked pot before, but he would now consider it. So, they included Ol' John in the passing of the joints. The pot wasn't that potent. Barry and Bobby were pot smokers, and this stuff was downright awful. It was harsh, rough on the throat, and had a negligible effect on them. And it definitely did little to curb Barry's nicotine addiction. Ole John, on the other hand, was getting pretty whacked. He started telling Bobby about how he was looking at "the world being upside down, where the ground was up and the moon was down" and a bunch of other babble. Yeah, Ole John was stoned for the first time and was experiencing all the things that go along with it, rising above the rattling and rocking of the boxcar in camaraderie with his new friends. *Damn schwag!*

After a while, the train had stopped on a sidetrack to allow another train to pass. They were now free to roam the side of the tracks where they could harvest in earnest. They ripped up a couple of plants by the roots, threw them into the boxcar, and fired up that ol' Sterno. Bobby removed the batteries from his flashlight and packed it full of pot. He later emptied it all out, knowing that it was too risky to have if they were entertained by the police again. Oh well. It temporarily put some needed smoke into Barry's lungs, but the stuff wasn't worth keeping.

In the middle of Iowa inside a stifling hot boxcar with no food in their stomachs other than a shared package of Reese's peanut butter cups and a can of potatoes, they were beginning to feel the pangs of hunger, but they were used to it. As soon as dusk became night, the conversation ebbed, and each exhausted rambler gave in to the rhythmic lull of the ride, the *cha chang, cha chang, cha chang* each time the wheels of the boxcar rolled over the expansion joints.

Throughout the night, the train wove its way toward hints of urbanized areas, leaving the dense agricultural earth behind. By early morning, the four vagabonds had arrived in the Cicero, Illinois yard, the end of the line for this leg of the journey.

Before departing from the train John told Barry and Bobby they would not be able to pick up an eastbound freight from the hub where they had just been dropped off. John added he would be able to hook them up with a place to eat and sleep, which gave the guys all the more reason to tag along. The gesture was a no-brainer, tired and hungry, they took the lead of their trusted friend. John's intention was to head to the Pacific Garden Mission in downtown Chicago, a walk of about seven miles. Before they left, Bobby had to wrap tape and twine around his boot to bind it together.

They walked through diverse neighborhoods, some friendly, some confused by their presence. Before long, they found themselves passing through a poor business district. The old sidewalk was grubby, with black-spotted circles of old gum, cigarette butts, and splashes of spittle. Old fading and peeling storefronts rose up four floors or so. People were bustling about, so they blended in with all the activity going on around them. They stepped up to the shaded side of a mom-and-pop grocery store to take a rest when Barry noticed a hose bib on the side of the building. This was an opportunity for him to fill up his canteen.

While everyone took turns splashing their faces and cupping their hands to drink deeply, they noticed a bread truck pulling into the loading zone in front of the store. The driver stepped out of the cab and walked around to open the back doors of the truck releasing the aroma of freshly baked bread. All eyes were focused on the driver as he reached in and pulled out trays of loaves of bread. For the four guys, the sight and smell was too much to bear in light of their empty stomachs.

Bobby lagged a few steps as the troop walked past the bread truck. Impulsively and as quick as a flash, he snatched a loaf of bread. He calmly walked down the sidewalk, away from the scene of the crime until he met with his companions. Bobby divided the loaf into four portions, and they all abetted in the crime by devouring the evidence. Amazing how something so simple can taste so good when one is really hungry.

It took around three hours to get from Cicero to downtown Chicago. John, having walked this path many times, knew the way to the mission, which was located at 646 South State Street on the west side section of Chicago. The area in the '70s was known to be frequented by homeless people. At a distance, they could see a quote taken from Roman 6:23 painted on the wall in huge black, red, and blue letters. There it was—a marquee that ran up the side of the building to the height of three floors that read "Pacific Garden Mission."

They arrived just in time for lunch. There was a crowd of mostly men congregating near the front entrance. John told them they needed to get in line if they had any hope of getting food and a bed. They stood in line with other hopefuls along with the regular downtrodden humans, most being drunks, druggies, or crazies. The gathering crowd was noisy with chatter, shouts of laughter, and arguments.

The door finally opened, and the crowd began to file in. Barry and Bobby soon learned that before being served food, they had to sit through a lengthy religious service that ended with former addicts and converts giving their testimony of conversion from their former lives to the renewed creatures that they were now. Bobby recalled:

Some of the testimonies were stirring. I could hear the sincerity in the voices of those who were convinced that they had been saved from whatever it was that they were running from or with.

The main worship hall had an overflowing crowd. Barry and Bobby sat on folding chairs in the hallway outside the worship hall and listened to the sermon on a speaker. Suddenly a fight broke out between two men in the hallway not far from where they were sitting. The brawlers were quickly set upon by a few other men who hustled them outside. Bobby remembered some of the lyrics being sung by a man giving his testimony on the stage "Love lifted me; love lifted me." It was a bit out of tune, but he sang it in earnest. Most of what was being said or sung fell on deaf ears. The crowd was here to get "fed and get a bed." The sermon was something that had to be tolerated to get to that end.

When the sermon was over the crowd instinctively stood and queued up again. This time the line wound down a flight of stairs to the basement where the food was being served. They would pass stations with a variety of food. A carton of white or chocolate milk. An about out-of-date Stewart sandwich. A cup of mulligan stew that had undercooked potatoes, carrots, and onions mixed into some kind of thickened goo. It was protein, and it was free.

Barry and Bobby would readily have eaten anything set before them. Barry recalled topping the meal with the weirdest cup of black coffee he had ever drunk. "It didn't even taste like coffee!" After gathering up all that was offered to them, they moved off to the dining room to eat. The dining room had long tables that extended the length of the room. There were no chairs, so they stood eating face-to-face with people on the opposite side of the table, shoulder to shoulder.

After Barry and Bobby finished eating, John played host and ushered them up two flights of stairs to the dormitory. Pathways between the cots were so narrow that you had to walk sideways to get down the rows.

John said, "On any given night you might see men sleeping off the alcohol, snoring, with limbs hanging over the sides of the small cots. Some men can be seen peeling off their clothing and putting them under their cots," he laughed, "or not peeling their clothing at all, being content to sleep as they were, fully clothed."

Barry and Bobby looked at each other and began to express their feelings about the place. John had warned them to be on guard. They recalled his words, "Sometimes bad things happen to people here after the lights go out." With those words, they felt the streets would be safer and decided to take their chances to find a freight train they could hop on.

Barry's experience in the mission gave way to his recollection of life in the Canadian hostels, away from the city, where he felt safe, was fed for work or for a small fee, and was surrounded by like-minded young travelers. The mission was no kin to the hostels.

In the afternoon they walked around to see where the nearest railyard was and were told where one could be found not too far away. They headed south and then west on one of the side streets, probably LaSalle. As they approached a bridge and looked down they could see tracks, but this didn't look like any freight yard they had ever seen. There were no boxcars, just lines of passenger cars. Adjacent to the bridge was a small building occupied by a rail worker who noticed the two guys.

Opening the door he said, "Can I help you guys?"

Barry and Bob related their story of the past forty-eight hours and how they were penniless and looking to hop a freight out of the city. They didn't have any other options. The man, taking in all the information, frowned. He took genuine pity on them and their situation and gave them five dollars. In '72, five dollars was a substantial amount of money.

"Look, you guys need to get outta here. Honestly, you won't survive the night." Pointing he added, "There's a bus station north of here on the corner of Randolph and Clark Streets."

They immediately started walking toward the bus terminal looking for a street heading north when they were stunned by the sight of rats the size of muskrats—runover, bloodied, dead—in the middle of the road. The hideous image of the dead rats was something they had never seen in any rural New England town.

They began to second-guess their decision to leave the mission as they trekked about a half a mile toward the Greyhound bus station. Good news! Well, they could go to Gary, Indiana for $2.50.

Bobby looked at Barry and said, "Gary, Indiana. Barry, that's a whole state away. That's one state closer to home. What do you think?"

They didn't have a clue as to where Gary, Indiana even was. If they had, they wouldn't have gone there. Gary, Indiana is the home of the Jackson Five. From March 10–12, 1972, the National Black Political Convention was held there.

"Yeah...give us two tickets for Gary, Indiana."

The bus wasn't leaving until five, giving Barry and Bobby time to chill. In spite of all the commotion going on, Barry was able to get an hour of needed sleep until the loudspeaker announced the bus was boarding for Gary, Indiana. With tickets in hand, they hurried to the bus. Barry and Bobby found the first available seats; aah... sighs of relief as they plopped down grateful to be leaving Chicago.

The forty-five-minute trip was routine and humdrum. The bus let them off on the curbside not far from Broadway and East Fourth Avenue. They were thrown an unexpected curveball when just as they stepped off the bus, they were approached by a half dozen Black teens of about sixteen or seventeen years old. Hmm... Here they thought they were leaving Chicago to find a safer place to sleep only to find that they were now in a more precarious situation.

Two white kids getting off the bus with backpacks in Gary. They had planned to walk to the bus station located at a storefront of a redbrick building, but as soon as they disembarked, the bus left, and they found themselves in front of locked doors. They had no idea which way to go but knew for certain they couldn't stand still. Their first consideration was to simply walk off and leave the group of guys behind. No chance. The group was following at their heels.

The most outspoken member looked at Barry and said, "Hey, how much is that shit that you're carrying worth?"

Barry replied, "Not much. We've already been robbed."

His response brought a chorus of laughter from the group. It was to the point that more than a few people driving by were jeering at them from car windows. These guys were not going to let Barry and Bobby go that easy.

Barry was not ready to do battle over a backpack and really thought these guys were messing with them. The group had the advantage; Barry and Bobby were definitely on their turf. Bobby was nervous and thought they meant to do them both bodily harm.

Still walking slowly with the group in tow, they came to the intersection of the two city streets. Bobby could see a white driver stopped for a red light and hoped he could get them out of their predicament. Bobby left the sidewalk and walked to the car.

The driver's window was down so he leaned into the car and said, "We're in a bad situation here"—motioning behind him— "Could you please, give my friend and me a ride, maybe even just around the corner?"

The man looked over to the sidewalk and then back to Bobby and said, "Okay, get in."

Bobby turned and yelled, "Come on, Barry!!"

Barry, relieved that he didn't have to continue his unsuccessful attempts at keeping his backpack, eagerly jumped in. The man drove a few blocks, took a left, stopped in front of a diner, and asked, "Are you guys hungry?"

"Yes!" was their reply.

"Okay...me too. I'll treat." They grabbed their backpacks, moseyed inside, and sat down at the booth closest to the restaurant window where they set their backpacks on the side.

Barry and Bobby sat down at the booth together, facing the rear of the diner and across from their newfound friend. The man introduced himself as Jim. He handed them both menus and said, "Go ahead, order something." Burgers, fries!! Neither guy could remember the last time they tasted a juicy burger with fries dipped in ketchup.

So, while waiting for their meal Jim took the opportunity to start a conversation and asked about their situation. This was a long story, both taking turns between mouthfuls of food telling him of their adventures hitching, hopping trains, and subsequently, the robbery. Barry started feeling uneasy about Jim. He didn't seem to approve of them, and it didn't make sense why he invited them into the diner.

While the conversation was going on, Barry noticed a waitress in the back of the diner standing in the doorway of a small room housing the restrooms. This was weird. She was staring at him and mouthing stuff he couldn't understand. As Barry was looking at the woman, Bobby held Jim's attention, so it wasn't obvious what was going on behind him. With all that had happened in the past few days all Barry could think of was that their newfound friend, Jim, might be a really bad guy! He had to find out and excused himself from the table saying that he had to go to the men's room.

Barry walked to the rear of the diner, about twenty feet. The woman by this time had slipped into the small area housing the restrooms. Barry rounded the corner and immediately saw her standing at the far wall with a fork in hand.

Before he could say anything, she blurted out in a loud raspy whisper, "I know you're talking about me! I know that you're talking about me and my witchcraft!"

This was the last thing Barry was expecting to encounter rounding that corner. What do you say to a woman with a fork who thinks you're talking behind her back?

"Hell no, not me!" Barry slowly stepped back keeping an eye on the waitress and hurried back to the table, not wanting to be part of someone's mental breakdown. He had his own issues and had reached his limit. He wanted out! Out of the diner, out from all the people and most of all, out of Gary, Indiana.

Barry approached the booth where Jim and Bobby were sitting and said "Bobby, I'm leaving." He grabbed his backpack and thanked Jim for the meal and headed to the entrance. Bobby, in turn, caught off guard and seeing the look in Barry's eyes did the same, exiting the diner.

Barry, standing roadside, looked to his right and could see the archway of an old round stone bridge, a railroad bridge about five hundred feet away. Instinctively, with little hesitation, they both hastily walked to what would be their salvation. They climbed an embankment encountering a steel fence that appeared to have been breached many times before from the bottom. Pushing their backpacks through the opening, Barry squeezed under first with Bobby's help holding up the bottom flap, careful to not let the bottom spikes grab Barry's body. Once through, Barry reciprocated. Both were now behind the fence and looking at the track fifteen feet away.

It was still light; the sun was starting to go down. The rail track ran east/west, so they took a right and started walking out of Gary in an easterly direction. Ideally, Barry and Bob were hoping that a train would come slow enough for the two to hop on but that didn't happen. To the north was the Gary Works steel mill, the city's largest employer at approximately thirty thousand and once considered the world's largest steel mill. North of the mill was the south end of Lake Michigan and south of the mill was urban Gary. The two continued walking late into the night as trains whipped by them at full speed.

Around midnight it started to drizzle, and they needed to find an area to settle in to protect everything from getting wet. Finding a grassy area about thirty feet from the tracks, Barry and Bob pulled out their sleeping bags covering themselves with the space blankets trying to get a few hours of sleep before morning.

Chapter 22

THE END OF THE ROAD

Bobby awoke to a drop of water dripping down into the palm of his open hand. He poked his head out into the dawn of a gray sky and advancing rain. They had to roll up quickly to keep the sleeping bags from getting too wet. With the sleeping bags secured to the bottom rack of their backpacks, they could cover themselves and backpacks with their ponchos and walk on. Nearing a spaghetti bowl at the highway intersections of I-65 and I-90, they kept walking until it was clear they were walking east on I-90. It was fast-moving traffic, and no one was going to stand on the brakes to stop and pick up two vagabonds thumbing in the breakdown lane.

Nonetheless, they walked with their backs to the traffic, thumbs out. Trudging forward, they eventually saw a rest area. After using the restroom, they walked back out into the parking lot and decided to walk on. In the section reserved for big trucks, there was a cabover trailer truck with the cab raised up. The driver was standing and staring at the engine compartment. Bobby, wandered by the truck and asked the truck driver if he minded if he could have a look.

"Sure." He extended his hand and said, "Name is Frank. Any help I can get is greatly appreciated."

It seemed the truck had developed an air leak that would not allow it to build enough air pressure to release the brakes. Upon close examination Bobby found the source of the leak. A braided air line running from the compressor had chafed through to the point that the thin remaining wall of the hose blew a bubble and it had popped, leaving a gaping hole that the air poured out of. The inside diameter of the blown-out hose was about the same size as the outside diameter of the aluminum frame of his backpack.

The first question Bobby asked was, "Do you have any tools?"

Frank answered, "I don't have much of a tool kit. I got a screwdriver, a pair of pliers, a file, and a pocketknife."

It was not much to work with but enough to do what he was planning to do. In the field of auto mechanics, Bobby was MacGyver before MacGyver was cool. First, he used the file to do the tedious job of cutting off about three inches of one side of his backpack, which caused his pack to lean to one side for the rest of the trip. He then cut the damaged hose a bit north and south of the breach and inserted the aluminum tube into the two open ends of the hose, forming a union.

To finish the task, he needed a couple of hose clamps to hold this union together. Thankfully, he found what he was looking for, but the operation of the heater would have to be sacrificed. Finally, he bypassed the heater hose out to the heater element and rounded it back to the water pump and salvaged the return line along with its two hose clamps for the union on the airline. Perfect! Worked like a charm.

"Fire it up, see if it will hold air," said Bobby.

The driver climbed up into the raised cabin and perched himself in the driver's seat. He rattled the shift around to put the truck in neutral, turned the key to the on position, and pushed the starter button. The old Detroit two-stroke sprang to life. Frank continued to sit in the driver's seat to watch the needle on the air pressure gauge.

Frank jumped out of the cab onto the ground and said, "Looks good! One hundred pounds and holding." Then he turned the lever and lowered the cab. Now relieved he asked, "Where ya you guys going, anyway?"

"We are heading home to Worcester, Massachusetts," replied Bobby.

"Look, I am on my way with this load of Budweiser. I can take you as far as Albany if you want to go. "

The guys said, "Sure."

"You guys wait here. I gotta make a phone call. "

Frank came back to announce, "The receiver said he will take the load late. If it wasn't for you, I would still be sitting here broken down for God knows how long. Let's get rolling."

The truck was an old cabover "Crackerbox Jimmy" with a screaming 318 Detroit and a 13-speed. Frank's CB handle was the Flying Turtle. It was painted in lettering on both sides of the truck. He was an owner/operator, one of the few occupations where you would start at the bottom and work your way down.

Bobby thoroughly enjoyed talking with him and studying him as he masterfully piloted his old truck. Meanwhile, Barry, who had zero interest in trucks took the opportunity to get some sleep. There was no power steering. Lock to lock of the steering wheel was about five turns. After completing a turn, the wheel would return to center on its own, spinning like a top, and slowed to a stop with gentle friction from his hand. His shifting was so precise that you would have sworn that he had an automatic. Frank explained and demonstrated how to shift without using the clutch and said, "It's all about timing and listening to the rpms of the engine."

The Flying Turtle drove all night to make up for lost time, and it was around 11:00 a.m. when Frank exited at a New York service plaza situated in the middle of the east- and westbound lanes on I-90.

"This is the end of the line, boys. I'm getting off at the next exit. I'm going to use the restroom and get a quick bite to eat. I think it would be better for you guys to hitchhike here as opposed to the entrance ramp where I will be getting off."

Bobby extended his hand, and replied, "It's alright, man."

Barry shook his hand and said, "Yeah, man. We appreciate the ride."

The two guys quickly headed to the fast-food restroom to relieve themselves and get cleaned up for their homeward journey. As they were walking out, Barry in the rear noticed a half-eaten burger lying unattended on the empty table. It had been nearly forty-eight hours since they had last eaten, and the sight of the lone burger was too tempting to resist. He grabbed the burger and in one bite it was gone. It hardly filled the void in his stomach but was worth the damage to his pride. When he caught up to Bobby, he told him of what he had just done. From the look on his friend's face, Barry could not tell if he saw envy or disgust.

Barry started searching the adjacent trash bins looking for a piece of cardboard. Maybe it was the half-eaten burger or just the realization they were only a few hours from getting home, but he had a new source of strength. He could almost smell the New England air with each breath. Finding what he figured was the best piece of cardboard under the circumstances, he pulled out his trusty Magic Marker. It had gotten them this far and it would get them home.

In large overly blackened letters, he wrote **WORCESTER**. From their location they could see the interstate on-ramp and started walking, but before making it there a man saw the sign, stopped, and yelled through the open window, "I'm heading to Boston. I'll be going close to Worcester."

Barry threw his backpack in the back seat of the '66 dark blue Rambler Classic along with Bobby and his stuff, and he jumped in the front.

Their driver's name was Seth, and he was heading to Boston to start his senior year at Brandeis University. His major was Business and he needed to get back for the beginning of the fall semester that started in several weeks. He was coming from the Adirondacks, where he had camped with friends to enjoy the last days of summer. Barry, hesitantly, told him he had just graduated with an associate's degree and wasn't sure what he wanted to do with his life.

While all this conversation was going on Bobby was in the back seat catching up on necessary sleep. He had been up the night before keeping Frank alert. It was only about three hours from Albany to Worcester, and the time went quickly telling Seth about their adventures hitching and hopping trains. There was that moment when they both regarded each other with envy.

Bobby woke up in the back seat and realized they were approaching Route 146. He had slept a few hours. Unlike most people, he seemed to work well with less sleep. They determined this would be the best location to be dropped off for the hitch to Holden.

From the back seat, Bobby said, "You can pull over here."

Seth maneuvered to a good spot on the side of I-90 (Mass Pike) and stopped. I-90 wasn't as busy as it is now, but still this transfer needed to be quick. They thanked Seth for the ride. Grabbing their packs they jumped the guardrail in front of them, negotiating the embankment to Route 146.

It was August 13, almost four weeks since they had set out on this journey, grabbing a ride to Montreal on a Peter Pan bus from Worcester, Massachusetts. The day was warm, bright blue sky with no clouds, not your usual New England day. The familiar sights and smells only added to their excitement. They were only thirty minutes from home.

Barry let out a deep breath and excitedly flipped the cardboard sign with Worcester boldly written on it and wrote **HOLDEN**. However, before Barry could hold out the sign, Bobby's extended thumb caught the eye of a passing driver, who pulled over to pick them up.

Seeing their bedraggled condition as well as their weathered backpacks he couldn't help but ask, "Where are you guys going with the backpacks and all?"

Bobby responded, "It's not that we are going somewhere, it's that we've been somewhere," and then added, "We're only a few miles away from home."

Barry and Bobby hopped in the car for their last ride home, and once again they began to relate highlights of their journey on the road.

Impressed, the driver said, "I'll tell you what. After what you guys have just been through, I think I can take you out of my way and drive you to Holden.

They continued telling their story all the way home where the driver dropped Barry off at the intersection of Main Street and Bailey Road. He thanked the driver and told Bobby he would give him a call later in the day. Little did Barry know this would be the last time he would ever hitchhike again. Not only did he not hitchhike, but he never picked up hitchhikers. He felt bad about that because he really wanted to trust people, but times were changing and after Wyoming he wouldn't take that chance again.

It was a one-mile walk from Main Street, down Bailey Road to his home on Dawson Pond (Cattail Cove), something he had done probably one hundred times in the past. It was normally a leisurely fifteen-minute walk, but Barry was in a hurry and cut a few minutes off that time. He was hungry and definitely needed a shower. What came first didn't matter. He was almost home...a hot shower, food, and a soft bed. Walking up the three-hundred-foot dirt road from Bailey to Cattail Cove, he could see the driveway was empty of vehicles...no one was home.

Barry walked up to the front door and gave the doorknob a turn, locked. It was unusual because his parents lived in a very secluded area, but he knew his dad was becoming more cautious. Barry only hoped the spare key was where they normally hid it. Luckily, it was, and Barry was inside in seconds.

Before continuing on, Bobby asked the driver, "Do you mind if I ride up front with you?"

"Not at all."

He drove the last few miles to the intersection of the road where Bobby lived and to the road that would take the driver to Paxton. So happy, he graciously thanked him for delivering them so close to home.

With a smile, he said, "Welcome home, young man."

With the sole of his boot taped on, Bobby walked the last mile to Alice's house where Christine would be waiting. He experienced a range of emotions from the joy of being home to the apprehension that Christine might have given up on him. He walked, taking in the surroundings. The odors of mid-August New England were so familiar—drying leaves, pine trees, newly mowed grass, the smell of the hot asphalt road.

He noticed things that he had never seen before like a stone wall, and a neighbor's house that had gone unnoticed. He was acutely aware of the sound of his own footsteps until at last, he stood at the end of the drive that led to Alice's front door.

Christine was in the front yard, walking toward the front door, having just picked a basket of asparagus. He called out her name. She turned to look at him, paused for a moment, and dropped the portable radio and basket she had been holding. They rushed to each other. For Bobby, this was so right, and he wondered, "How could I have been such a fool to wander away from her?"

Chapter 23

REFLECTIONS IN
THEIR OWN WORDS

Barry

THE HOUSE WAS EMPTY, EVERYONE was gone, but that didn't matter. First thing...check out the refrigerator and see what's available. I made myself three fried eggs, over easy and toast to sop up the running yoke. It was a beautiful day. My parents owned a Swiss-style chalet that overlooked Dawson Pond and I stepped out onto the upper deck and looked out over the view that surrounded me. I was happy to be home, having accomplished a trip from Nebraska to Massachusetts on only $2.50. Thinking back, maybe it would have been wiser to call home and try to have money wired for me and Bobby to take a bus. That would have been the smart thing, but I was a stubborn teenager and didn't want to ask my parents to bail me out.

In the following weeks, it became more apparent to me that my life had changed because I had changed. I had just celebrated my twentieth birthday, which gave me pause to think about what I wanted. I knew life was fragile and no day was guaranteed. Wanting to do something more with my life, I decided a Liberal Arts associate's degree was not enough and I needed to continue my education.

With education foremost on my mind, I went back to my former job at the college bookstore. This was a good start because I could work full-time during the day and take advantage of free classes offered to employees at night. I even made a deal where I could sit in on some day classes not offered at night and fill in that time as a lunch break. I was becoming a professional student! I met my future wife unexpectedly one day. As I was leaving the bookstore and merging into the hallway with people heading in both directions, I literally bumped into Celeste. It was one of those moments. We started talking and realized we were both going to the school auditorium for one of their weekly fun presentations. I asked if she would like to accompany me. She said, "sure."

In that short time, we both became aware of our mutual attraction to one another. Celeste would eventually move in with me in the downstairs apartment on Dawson Pond that I rented from my parents. She had her own room and now I didn't need to drive to Blackstone every week to see her. I would take my '70 Honda CB350 to work, and she would drive my '66 AMC Rambler Ambassador to school. She worked at a local restaurant on weekends and helped my mom with housework, and we all sat down every day at the dinner table.

I've always believed my cross-country adventure helped mold me in becoming the person I had now become. I had direction and goals. Celeste gave me a reason for everything. She has always been my muse.

After ten years of working toward building our careers, fixing our old dilapidated ten-thousand-dollar house, and learning to be self-sufficient, we were ready to bring our son, Seth—who continues to make us proud—into the world in '83.

Bobby and I were still very close friends, both enjoying scuba diving together. He and Chris moved to Florida and within a few years he gave Celeste and me an offer we couldn't refuse. The offer: he would move me down with his tractor trailer and Christine would build me a house across from theirs.

Christine had become successful in real estate. The Bobby and Barry adventures would continue including scuba diving in the state of Florida, Dry Torugas, and Bahamas!

On January 18, 2024, Celeste and I celebrated our fiftieth wedding anniversary. I've never regretted a moment of our lives together.

Bobby

In a month's time, I would begin to put my life into working order. The threat of the witch at the draft office years prior haunted me. To put this behind me, I joined the army, which instilled discipline and provided me with a trade that I would employ after my hitch. On New Year's Eve in '72, I married Christine. It's been fifty-one years since that event. It was the best decision I have ever made.

My desire for wanderlust was still strong; however, my partner this time would be my life mate, Christine. The army sent us to Washington State for a year and then off to Germany for two more. When I was off duty or on leave, we traveled to many European countries. I was even able to convince her to hitchhike around England with me. After the army, I pursued the trade for which the army trained me. I became an over-the-road trucker. It was a demanding trade, but it satisfied my desire for travel, it paid reasonably well, and I had wheels under me that would take me home.

In the years that followed, we started a family—a girl, Miranda, and soon after a boy, Jesse. Both have grown to lead productive lives with gainful occupations, a nurse and a police officer, with families of their own.

EPILOGUE

FEBRUARY 2024 MARKED THE ANNIVERSARY of when I first began my own three-year journey writing about Barry and Bobby's cross-country trip through Canada and the United States. I got to witness first-hand how their friendship evolved through their youthful stories and years of living well into the autumn of their lives.

They have become pretty much inseparable even as the cleft caused by their political divide made it more challenging to remain friends. I believe that if it wasn't for their coming together to write this book, their divide might have deepened. Reviving their long-stored memories to fill the pages helped them to realize all their years together were more important than politics.

After all, when they returned from their trip in August of '72, Barry was called upon to be Bobby's best man when he married Christine, and Bobby became our son's godfather when Seth was born in '83. As time churned forward, the two eventually became four and then seven. Barry and Bobby became scuba diving buddies. Each year we would spend a week in July vacationing either in cabins at Loblolly Cove in Rockport, Massachusetts or in a big house in York, Maine where they would take their tanks and go lobstering.

In '86 Bobby, Christine, and their two children moved to Florida to be closer to her father. No doubt the weather had something to do with it too. After a few visits, we began toying with the idea of moving to Florida, and by '87 we had made our decision. Bobby and Christine made the move so easy. She began dabbling in real estate, procuring a lot for us across the street so she was able to oversee the building of our house; Bobby used his eighteen-wheeler to move all our belongings to our new house. They were our friends and neighbors. Life was fun for all of us—sharing meals, holiday festivities, and outdoor activities like boating, picnicking, and, of course, scuba diving. They have since moved to the next town ten minutes away, but we still live in our original Florida home.

The only constant is change. Barry and Bobby's relationship has changed, but their friendship remains deep-rooted in the experiences shared exclusively by them.

ACKNOWLEDGEMENTS

My fortuitous, unplanned meeting with a stranger led me to the path of publication. On the spur of the moment, Robin Slotnick, a good friend, asked if I would like to join her and an acquaintance for a drink. Little did I know that the woman I was about to be introduced to is the talented novelist, Katherine MK Mitchell, whose latest book *From Budapest to Hollywood* was published earlier this year. She seemed keenly interested in my story and was instrumental in getting my editor and publisher, Cheryl Benton, and for that I am beyond grateful. After Ms. Mitchell contacted her, I was surprised to find an email from Cheryl a few days later, letting me know that she was willing to read my manuscript. Months later, she offered to work with me and publish the book. Cheryl's guidance and support throughout the editing and publishing process have been second to none. Kudos to you, my friend.

I appreciate all the support Christine Young has given us. After all, she had to give up her husband every Tuesday. She was the only one who knew about our long-drawn-out writing experiment and kept it mum. For three years, I didn't discuss the book with anyone for fear that something would happen, and the book would never come to fruition.

Many thanks to Theresa Wilkinson, English teacher, and editor extraordinaire, for being the first to read my manuscript when it was completed. Editing with Theresa brought a lightness to the task as we pored through the pages drinking coffee and eating Danish. We were only ten chapters into the third edit before Cheryl Benton took on full responsibility for the book.

I would like to recognize my good friends, Naomi Baldwin and Joni Rose, for their encouragement and the hours we spent laughing and reminiscing about our own lives in the '70s. Jeanne Crepeau, thanks for pushing me forward. Susie Whitaker, you will always be my endearing "staughter."

I must acknowledge the Johnson and Young children: Miranda, Jesse, and Seth, who entertained and challenged us by creating their own adventures through the years. And I would be remiss if I didn't mention my sister Diane Gauthier's daughters, Andrea and Natalie, who became my "naughters" after her death. Natalie, thank you for teaching me everything I know about outlines and more importantly Google Docs.

Cheers to Barry Johnson and Bobby Young!

ABOUT THE AUTHOR

Celeste Gauthier Johnson has spent over forty years teaching reading and language arts to middle-schoolers. Her forte has always been working with struggling readers, especially students with dyslexia. She has a Master of Arts degree in English from Assumption University in Worcester, Massachusetts. The narrative memoir about her husband, Barry, and his friend Bobby is her first published work. She currently lives in Florida and enjoys the vegetable garden and beautiful landscape Barry has created.

www.ingramcontent.com/pod-product-compliance
Lightning Source LLC
Chambersburg PA
CBHW071156130626
46553CB00004B/1681